JOYFUL
IN THE SILENCE

*The Making of a
Casual American Contemplative*

Books by Marsha Sinetar

Dreams unto Holiness
Ordinary People as Monks & Mystics, Revised (2007)
Don't Call Me Old, I'm Just Awakening
Sometimes, Enough is Enough
Spiritual Intelligence
The Mentor's Spirit
Holy Work
Reel Power
To Build The Life You Want, Create The Work You Love
Developing a 21st Century Mind
Living Happily Ever After
A Way Without Words
Elegant Choices, Healing Choices
Do What You Love, The Money Will Follow
Ordinary People as Monks & Mystics (1985)

Gift & Children's (Illustrated) Books

Why Can't Grown Ups Believe in Angels?
Self-Esteem is Just An Idea We Have About Ourselves
A Person is Many Wonderful, Strange Things

Monographs From T h e C e n t e r***

Can You Simply Trust?
Posture of Heart Series, I *(Preview)*
Posture of Heart, II *(The Mary Pattern)*
Posture of Heart, III *(Practice: Inclining the Ear)*
Posture of Heart, IV *(Contemplative Study)*
Dreams Unto Holiness *(Inquiry Series, #1)*

***Center publications as limited R & D works, may be **unavailable.**

JOYFUL
IN THE SILENCE

*The Making of a Casual
American Contemplative*

MARSHA SINETAR

FIRST EDITION

Library of Congress (c) 2021

Cover design: Kerry Watson

ISBN: 978-0-9661801-0-7

"Sir," said Caspian, "will you tell us
how to undo the enchantment which
holds [these people] asleep?"

"I will gladly tell you that, my son,"
said the Old Man. "To break this enchantment, you
must sail to the World's End, or as near to it as you
can, and you must come back having left one of
your company behind."

"And what is to happen to that one?" asked
Reepicheep.

"He must go on unto the utter east and never return
unto the world."
    "That is my heart's desire," said Reepicheep.

C.S. Lewis, *The Voyage of the Dawn Treader*

Dedication

I'm writing about events from a far distant vantage point. I've done my utmost to objectively describe my darling family, and long-gone, formative years. Several exceptional others became family. Youngsters, teachers, headmasters, my parents' friends cared for me. They guided me toward the good, and generously enriched my entire life.

I dedicate this book to my family of birth, and to my stand-in mothers, fathers, sisters, brothers. These good shepherds watched over me when I was young. I am more thankful than words can express. May God richly bless them all. I also dedicate this book to the loving memory of Raymond J. Sinetar, always in my heart.

ॐ

TABLE OF CONTENTS

PREFACE

"Here in silence is the Holy Wilderness, because the wilderness and the building of God are one." —Max Picard[1]

Every true contemplative is called into the Holy Wilderness. Its enriching silence explains why I live in a cloister of sorts, an inner reality that has become the crux and summit of my life. My autobiography would be invalid, incomplete, without telling of how I came to be a "casual contemplative"—relaxed, informal, but never indifferent. The world is full of tribulation; but here, in *the* Silence, one is ever infused with a quiet, peculiar joy.[2]

Unlike many lay contemplatives, I'm not affiliated with a religious order.[3] Nor do I follow the Rule (or life plan) of a designated saint. My routines loosely mirror those adopted by the solitary, spontaneously passionate, third century desert monks and mystics. Namely, they lived usually alone, in silence and utter simplicity, without an orderly dogma. (That came later.) They craved conscious *relationship* with God, aiming to live Christ. Their redirected focus was so "...all-embracing, because there is nothing that is outside it." Thus did their desert bloom.[4]

---

1. Max Picard, *The World of Silence* (Southbend, IN: Regnery/Gateway, 1952), 19.
2. Marsha Sinetar, *Sometimes, Enough is Enough* (NY: St. Martin's Press, 2007).
3. See for e.g. International Association of Lay Cistercian Communities; a worldwide contemplative movement.
4. Sr. Benedicta Ward, *The Wisdom of the Desert Fathers* (Fairacres, Oxford: SLG Press, 1981), vii.

These days, my life revolves around similar elements: prayer, study and meditation; silence and work (generally experienced as service, devotion, "charity" or love.) I've forged an ongoing modification of life known as "conversion of manners."[5] Unceasing *interior* prayer is the essence of any and all contemplative life, whether "casual" or cloistered. Furthermore, contemplative prayer is "the only *real* prayer" since it leads us beyond words (vocal prayer) and thought (meditative prayer), into the *reality* to which words and thought only point."[6] I shall repeat this point variously.

Here is the *key*: Only God calls us to any vocation, be it as a contemplative, or what have you. Conventional contemplatives live in a monastic setting, officially organized to support a life of solitude, prayer, meditation, work, and sometimes—even today—"mortification."[7] There are also whole communities of lay contemplatives, and independent casual contemplatives like me who live and practice mostly alone. The independent types hear no less of a spiritual call than the monastics, but may live and work more conventionally.

A journalist acquaintance fits the more casual profile: She works for a national organization, yet uses her day's free times for traditional contemplative practices. Another professional longs for solitary life, and waits for his children to grow so that he can set that up. I believe many artists, chefs, poets, inventors, leaders, and most highly focused individuals

---

5. Thomas Merton, *Cistercian Contemplative Spirituality,* July, 1991, Pamphlet, No pub. data.

6. Father J.Borst, MHM, *A Method of Contemplative Prayer* (Bombay, India: Asian Trading Corporation, 1975), 37.

7. For an explanation of contemplative life see: www.encylopedia.com.

are naturally contemplative. Unless their concentrations are part of some spiritual engrossment, their experiences could be simply related to their worldly enchantments. My narrative of such ideas is hardly exhaustive, and centers around autobiographical themes.

Many men and women construct their own cloister, yet live and work "independent of canonical status..."[8] If they could, many *more* would choose these "casual" routines–meaning, they'd follow a self-styled, worshipful, and no less sanctified life than that of those devoted to the radical move of the soul turned to God. It's rarely an easy choice, but for some of us, it's crucial.

The French monk, Abhishiktananda (born Henri Le Saux) wrote that the contemplative's healing function among us is so vital as to be indispensable to our collective welfare: Society should dedicate a percentage of itself (like a tithe) to that prayerful life, so that the Spirit within our ranks might be renewed by those who sit "in silence in the Presence and divine mystery *from which there is no return.*"[9]

In what follows, I offer no utopian or formulaic tips for the "good life." Like God's presence, my spirituality is *alive*, seems written on my heart, in the same way that some parents, healers, statespersons or truck drivers know their life is divinely right for them. Experientially , Cistercian, perhaps Benedictine, spirituality seems closest to my own. At least to this point, I've joined no group. (As should be clear, I've been thrown out of a few.)

---

8. ibid.
9. Abhishiktananda (Henri Le Saux) *Prayer* (Kashmir, Delhi: ISPCK, 1994), 68. Italics are mine.

Because even casual contemplatives pray and think deeply about eternal truths, I've been immersed in the study of Scripture, and the notions of the saintly, for a near lifetime. As a result, I've mooched a mode of living from, mostly, the desert fathers, integrating that with my otherwise secular life of teaching, writing, and domesticity. For the ancient monks the *goal* was God (i.e., living intimacy or union), and the way was Christ. The *spirituality* of the desert (or the wilderness, or set-apart life) is "not a *systematic* way, but full of hard work, experience, and prayer..." Prayer for such as the desert monks and mystics was neither tidily or tightly organized, nor was it a corporate affair; prayer wasn't ritualized. It was *not* an activity lasting a few moments or hours on a Sunday. "[It was] a *life continually turned to God.*"[10] Early on, reading such principles, I knew that was a universal path. And that it was meant for me.

With maturity, that inner prompt became urgent. Like Reepicheep in the opening quote, my heart's desire crystalized. Contemplative life seemed perfect. Was it, I wondered, too odd or too"set apart" for an ordinary person like me? 1 Peter 2:9, earlier still in Deuteronomy 14:2, explained my decision:

God calls believers, both Christians and Jews, to belong to Himself as " a peculiar people," to be His Own.[11] That's me. Such belonging felt right: My joy was and is of that sort, that variety, that Nature.

---

10. Benedicta Ward, *Wisdom of the Desert Fathers* (Fairacres, Oxford: SLG Press, 1981), xii, (italics, mine).
11. W.E. Vines, *Expository Dictionary of New Testament Words* (Nashville, TN: Thomas Nelson), lists "peculiar" under his definitions of the word "possession."

I call myself an *"American"* contemplative, because as a nation, we're inventive, and in true entrepreneurial fashion, any of us who are *casual* contemplatives must invent our life-path, listening inwardly for God's prompt and sacred will. We simply do the best we can.

How to shape and arrange such a life when one is, initially, less single-minded than, say, the desert fathers? And seeks approval, and longs to fit in? [12]

Therein rests my tale.

■

How did I come to *want* such a thing? As noted, I felt the divine prompt. Also, for openers, I also ask you to consider the orbit from whence I emerged: Shanghai, during a great, and truly devastating war.

Shanghai means "City by the Sea." Resting at the mouth of the Yangtze River, by the mid-1800s Shanghai was the county seat of the region. By the early 1900s it was an international hub of enterprise.

In the thirties, as a bustling cosmopolitan city, Shanghai had several distinct foreign settlements: British, French, Russian, American, Australian, Middle Eastern, and more. Today Shanghai ranks as one of the busiest container shipping ports globally.

My parents relocated to Shanghai, from Japan, before World War II broke out, before the Japanese occupation, when it was hospitable to all manner of different ideas, people, and

---

12. To "shape and arrange" in this context is a phrase I believe coined by scholar John Briggs.

cultures. That openness perfectly portrays my parents, my entire family, their friends. Such was the spirited democratic household into which I came. Our little nest was loving, creative, refined, gregarious. As for me, generally (not always) life was full of a radiant, if unseen, inexpressible Presence. Which made all the difference.

My parents on their wedding day.

☙

PART I

BEFORE FIVE

My father and me, in Shanghai.

My mother and Anthony, my brother, in Shanghai.

Chapter 1

THE SHANGHAI YEARS

The Lord possessed me in the beginning of His way,
Before His works of old, I was set up from everlasting,
from the beginning, or ever the earth was.
—**Proverbs 8:22 (KJV)**

In the mid-1930s, my father, Nathan ("Nat") and my
mother, Yvette, met and married in Kobe, Japan. My
father, an American entrepreneur in his early thirties, was
living in Japan for business—the import-export of natural
resources such as teak, steel, coal, and the like.

My mother had traveled to Kobe to visit her older
sister who then lived in Japan, with her American husband. My parents moved to Shanghai before the War, and
before China became a Communist country.

Shanghai, like Kobe, was a flourishing international
port. Since the late 1800s it had been home to a growing
number of foreign settlers, so was lively and cosmopolitan.

Dad was of Russian, or Lithuanian-Jewish, descent.
I'm told that, decades earlier, his father had immigrated to
America in his teens, by himself. My grandfather was possibly only seventeen. He traveled by ship, along with
crowds of immigrants from Eastern Europe. Many of these
migrants signed on to be indentured servants or laborers in
the U.S. My father's father may have been one.

In the mid-1800s, widespread famine in Lithuania
and shortages of basic resources in other Baltic countries

caused a mass migration to America. Latvians, Lithuanians, Poles, and Russians settled on the East Coast—in New York, and in Pennsylvania for instance—forced by circumstances to flee their homes and farms for work in U.S coal mines and factories.

I was told that my dad's father settled in New York, became an American citizen, worked like a dog, and prospered. When a distant cousin of my dad's traced their ancestry, she asked if I knew anything about our grandfather's history, or perhaps a story about my father's early life. I didn't.

My mother's past is even more mysterious. She was born in Cairo, Egypt to an Italian father, and (I think) a British-Italian mother. My mom was the youngest of eight children, half of whom died in childhood. She was raised at a Catholic school-and boarded in a Catholic convent. Was she ever a practicing Catholic? She evaded all talk of her youth. At the very least, hers was a Catholic "sensibility," and for better or worse, she was deeply affected by her upbringing. (Personally, I've always had a profound affinity with the mystical and contemplative aspects of the Roman Church, and cannot remember a time when I did not pray to God, and love the Catholic saints.)

My parents and grandparents on both sides of the aisle had few, if any, pictures taken. I've never seen a photo of my mother as a girl. And only one, rather somber, perhaps forlorn, looking Nathan as a youngster. When I see that picture of my dad, a mix of love, respect, and deep concern overwhelms me. I want to cry and always wonder what his boyhood had been like. His mother, my grandmother, Lily (*Mémère* to us all), was a mild, loving, considerate woman. I can't imagine her as a source of grief to her children—two sons—both of whom were devoted to her.

My dad, Nathan, as a boy.

My grandmother, Mémère, lived with us in my pre-school years. She was my best friend, confidant, and spiritual mentor. Mémère, a mix of piety and playfulness, was the sort to eat juicy mangoes while in the tub. She took me to every sort of church—Jewish, Catholic, Buddhist, and more. She recited Bible verses by heart about, say, David or Abraham, telling me, "You are Abraham's daughter, his seed, his heir." If troubles came, her mantras were, "This too shall pass," "It came *in order to pass*," and with a droll shrug, "Who'll know in a hundred years?" Mémère possessed a "let-it-be," Taoist attitude that I wish I could match. Like my dad, mom, and brother, my grandmother was funny—in a wry, understated, eye-rolling way.

My dad's father may have been tough, given his own difficult youth. Was my dad brow-beaten at home by a disciplinarian father? Was he bullied or persecuted at school for being Jewish? I pray not, but will never know. My erudite, philosophical father kept himself to himself. As I soon learned to do.

Neither of my parents had any appetite for organized religion. My mother discouraged any talk of religious ideas. One imagines that prior to World War II, politics and religion were touchy, if not forbidden subjects in the well-mannered social circles in which my parents traveled, in which they expected me to travel. I was taught *not* to discuss any such topics; something I've apparently chosen to ignore. Having been born with what's termed "the religious impulse," I tend to blurt out certain revelations to those who'd no doubt prefer not to hear them. So be it.

Mémère was my only source of spiritual support and encouragement. After age five—my dividing line—I was on my own.

EVERYONE'S FROM SOMEWHERE ELSE

Our household was colorfully global. Everyone thought in and spoke different languages. Mine included "body language" which could explain my close ties to so many unorthodox types. Wordlessly one can be kindred spirits. For example, to me, strangers often feel like relatives, and quickly become pals of a sort. In school, friends were whiz kids and ruffians; I loved them all, and especially enjoyed moving freely between groups. That's still the case.

"Live and let live" was the motto around our genial, variegated lair. My favorite uncle—Albert—used to say, "Everyone's from somewhere else." I sensed we empathized with the delight, dismay, and strangeness of being flawed and all too human.

OUR MULTI-LINGUAL CREW

My Shanghai family had a youthful heart. My parents,

grandmother Mémère, Anthony—my older brother by about seven years—Madame Paulynine, (my governess, whom I called "Madame,"), an *amah*[13] or two, our cook, and several domestic helpers—who cared for the house, the grounds, and a wide range of animals—was "family." My mother's only brother, Albert, may have lived with us then. He was the sweetest, jolliest uncle a child could have. For instance, if anyone—especially a child—broke or dropped something, Uncle Albert would call out gaily, "*Bravo! Aviva! Complimenti!* That's very good luck." If he was near, he'd pat us on the back vigorously. He was broke, but ever laden with little trinkets for Anthony and me.

I can't recall if my father's brother, Roger, lived with, or near, us. He was urbane, brainy, serious; like my dad, also in business. We lost touch after the War, when Mémère went to live with him in Europe and elsewhere.

My dad was schooled in England and was quite "British." He'd lived in the Far East for years. He and Anthony spoke Mandarin, Cantonese, a smattering of Japanese, and were both fluent in French. He understood Russian and Italian. My mother spoke Arabic, French, Italian and English. She thought in French and Italian, charmingly mixing these languages when she spoke. She addressed me in French, which I understood. Despite her lovely accent, and soft, melodic voice, I eventually asked her to speak to me only in English so that I could be "American." After arriving in the U.S., I didn't answer if spoken to in French.

At the time of my birth, Anthony lived away in boarding school, but returned home when the War broke out in

---

13. *Amah*—a female nursemaid, a baby's nurse, especially of Chinese origin. (See Merriam-Webster Dictionary, www.mirriamwebster.com).

the Pacific. My grandmother, Mémère, and my governess, Madame, lived with us until the War ended. They both spoke Russian, French, and English.

My brother, Anthony – world's cutest baby.

Until five years old, I spoke Russian fluently, understood French, although I could only read in English. After coming to America, I never spoke another word of Russian, and instantly extinguished my British accent. (Most of my playmates were English, and most schools I attended when we traveled—and tutors—were British.)

THE HIGH PRICE OF WAR

Eventually, around 1943, my father was escorted, at gunpoint, to a Japanese prisoner of war camp. Hazy images of that trauma remain: serious, young, raven-haired soldiers in khaki uniforms carrying rifles stand in our living room. Our entire household, including the servants, huddle together silently.

My parents' faces are ashen; my father, motionless, stands ramrod straight; my mother's cold, trembling hand grips mine. Anthony is crying; the soldiers talk quietly to my father. Then: seeing them touch his arm, I erupt.

Family lore has it that, as it came time for my dad to leave, I begin to fret. I vaguely recall lunging at the soldiers, arms swinging, trying to hit them, wanting to protect my father. My mother, horrified, says, "No, *Mon Choux*, no."[14] She pulls me away. Now everyone is crying. Except the soldiers. They stroke my hair, and smilingly talk to each other.

Years later, my mother admitted her terror. "I was afraid that they'd shoot you. They were *boys*, just boys doing their duty. They laughed at the thought of a tiny child trying to fight them. They only wanted to touch your white curls—so unusual, so odd to them."

My dad's absence depleted us. The entire household lost vitality. It was quieter. Everyone spoke less; Madame and Mémère grew ever more inward. One of them said, "There's always a price to pay in war. This one will really cost us." How true: We paid dearly.

My mother went into shock, then seemed to leave us. If I had to pinpoint it, that's when she and I drifted apart. The first door she shut was her attention. She could not focus when we spoke to her. Where was she?

I'd repeat, "Mummy, are you listening?" She'd reply, "*Oui, Mon Choux,* I heard you." But she hadn't. If Mémère

---

14. Literally, this means "my cabbage," but in French the phrase is used as an endearment for "my darling," or "my dear one," etc.

was present, she'd twist her mouth to one side, gaze steadily into my eyes, saying telepathically, "Don't fuss; leave her alone." If Madame was around, she'd calmly take my hand, lead me out of the room, softly suggesting, "Let's go read." One day, someone said, "Try to understand. Your mother, down deep in her soul, she is troubled." That was the only explanation given.

FORMATIVE INFLUENCES

Friends ask, "*Was that when you began to pray?*" and "*Who influenced you to pray?*" I can't remember a time when I didn't pray. But it was wordless—not like our familiar petition prayers.[15] Even in infancy, I felt a Someone within, a "vibe" of comfort and Companionship, ever present, with me. As will be clear, my grandmother supported my spiritual life, but God Himself authored my religious impulse. I believe that with the least encouragement, nearly every toddler would pray, for "...the kingdom of God belongs to children."[16]

In the Middle Ages, those with a religious call were thought to evolve, their faith developing with maturity. A child could be "dedicated" by parents to a monastery. I was not meant for formal cloistered life. If anything, as later chapters detail, I was programmed to be married with children, a blossom in the buttonhole of traditional womanhood. Life had other plans.

Artist Georgia O'Keeffe apparently loved (and remembered) the colors of her crib's bedding. In my crib, I adored God, invisible but wholly present. Prayer was like a steady

---

15. For more about this, visit YouTube, Marsha Sinetar/A Casual Contemplative's Archive, *Contemplative Prayer.*
16. Mark 10: 13-16

pulse—as it must be in all those with a religious instinct. Even very young children have an awareness of God, or *the Reality to which thought and words can only point.*[17] That's contemplative prayer, which seemed to develop spontaneously as an inborn grace. No one taught it to me. It goes on by itself, faint when I'm with people; wonderfully clear when alone. My experience is mild compared to the stories (hagiography) of saintly children . Such intense interiority often create conflicts between parents and their "old soul" youngsters.[18]

My father's imprisonment aside, before five, I felt surrounded by love. Our relatively easy life during the war, Memere and Madame's protectiveness, the whole household's sweetness toward my mother—all that felt blessed. The sympathetic nature of my family for those who were, at the time, enemies, shaped my own wish to forgive. How could any child, brought into the world by the divine love, not develop some sort of similar spiritual sensibility?

HOW LIFE WENT ON

Despite the War, my father's absence, our anxiety about him, and our constant need to hide in the bomb shelter, I loved living in Shanghai. The Chinese people around us were bright, caring, courteous. We lived in the British sector where people seemed considerate of one another . There was a close, village feeling.

Another plus: Anthony now lived with us. Although he was older, we got along and didn't argue too much. We

---

17. Father J. Borst's definition, from a pamphlet now out of print, that I've repeatedly cited previously.
18. D. Weinstein, R. Bell, *Saints and Society* (Chicago/London: University of Chicago Press, 1982).

Me – about age four.

had a lot of animals. There were horses nearby that one could ride. I rode constantly on one that was "mine". Until my teens, God, books and horses were my great loves. (After that, books and boys ranked high, with God as my most private, unexpressed, Friend.)

Animals were a constant: ours included two German Shepherds (more watchdogs than pets), several cats, chickens, goats, occasional baby goats (unbelievably cute and playful) and—regrettably—a gaggle of aggressive, territorial geese.

THE ADVERSARIAL GOOSE

Once, while playing outdoors, a gray goose with reddish, reptilian eyes thought I was invading its pond. It went berserk. Flapping its wings madly, it honked, flew out of the water , then charged at me. I raced to the house in a panic, opened and shut the front door *just* as the foul thing's beak caught up with my legs. Beware the furious birds.

Three memories linger menacingly from those Shanghai days: (1) my dad's ordeal during the insanity of war; (2) low-flying planes, dropping bombs nightly within earshot of our home; (3) that goose-attack.

The upshot? One learns early to avoid the disturbed.

ॐ

A rare moment with my mother.

The delights of absorption

My dear Memere

Chapter 2

THREE TEACHERS, BOOKS, AND FAREWELL

Georgia began to play apart from other children at a very young age...Later [she] remembered being happy keeping to herself.[19]
—Laurie Lisle

In Shanghai, home-school was a given. I doubt if any of my neighborly playmates—mostly British—attended regular schools. The conditions of war were such that I never went to either kindergarten or first grade away from home. After the War, before we left Shanghai, I recall being enrolled in some missionary school; they sent me home the very first day for refusing to say that I was a "shameful sinner". Generally obedient, that type of expulsion seemed my norm; it occurred repeatedly in childhood. (I've come to expel myself when situations feel unsuitable.)

Everyone in our household was teaching and, no doubt, learning all the time. While my brother, Anthony, had his tutor, each of the women in our family had her own expertise. So my primary education was rich and, believe me, constant. There were no grades, per se. Kindergarten and first grade melded into one. Even after we left Shanghai, I was either taught at home by a tutor, or

---

19. Laurie Lisle, *Portrait of an Artist, A Biography of Georgia O'Keeffe* (New York: Washington Square Press, 1980), 10.

enrolled in parochial schools. Not until sixth grade did I step into a public school. What a shock.

The lines of study just fell into a goodly, quite obvious place. There was no tug-of-war between the major players. Or so I assume. And if, perhaps, I was *too* well attended, the future took care of that.

My refined, enchanting mother dealt with the social graces; my grandmother saw to spiritual formation; Madame ruled academics. And pretty much everything else. She taught me to read, and by three I was devouring classical children's fare: Fables, fairy tales, a child's Bible stories, some fiction. It was fine prose—not picture books with the same, idiotic word on every page. The stories I read held *ideas* a child could chew on, and a sturdy vocabulary. Unlike the dumbed-down, over-engineered language offered to the young these days, Madame insisted on time-honored children's literature, with values that "trained up a child."

PLEASE MEET MADAME

Madame occupied the bulk of my time. Next to my father and grandmother her calm, sober individualist's influence on me was huge. She hadn't much humor, but the rest of us were comic enough to compensate.

Being extraordinarily forthright, she'd say, "Look people straight in the eye. Be honest, be punctual, be neat." (The latter virtue I have yet to master.)

Anthony, who was all-knowing about the adult world, told me Madame was a former Russian aristocrat. One never knew the source of his intelligence gathering. Both Anthony and my mother were excellent yarn-spinners, loved stories about people (much more than ideas), and

16

Anthony , before I was born.

seemed to prefer fictions over facts. Yet, that account about Madame was plausible. Her composure, regal bearing, obvious depth and breadth of knowledge spoke volumes about a noble, well-educated mind.

As my brother spun it, Madame had lost everything— husband, home, wealth, social standing—in some Bolshevik[20] uprising. I never got the story straight. Refined austerity and an iron will must have helped her weather her storms of family and financial devastation. Like my dad, she kept herself to herself. I, for one, would not have dreamt of asking her any personal questions.

Neither Anthony nor I knew how Madame found her way to us. Whatever her path, she blessed all our lives richly.

---

20. The Bolsheviks were a Russian political group that later became the Communist Party. In 1917, their famous revolt against the Tsar and ruling classes (a. k. a.: Red October) eventually resulted in Russia becoming the first socialist state.

A SORT OF MONTESSORI SYSTEM

We were a musical family.

"What shall we read today?" That was Madame's morning question, involving me—as a learner—in each day's lessons. I suspect she'd been influenced by the Italian physician, Dr. Maria Montessori, who believed that all children start out eager to learn.

Madame's methods were engaging. Naturally, instruction was completely individualized—no grade levels, per se; no fixed curriculum. Teaching followed my pace and ability to learn; lessons grew out of my enthusiasms. Madame inspired my lifelong love of learning, the deep desire to share that spark with others.

If my interests ran to cooking, Madame supervised as I baked cookies. Such methods could make a student rebellious, later on—when rules and regulations are required. Home schooling suggests otherwise.

Attempting new things—like baking—taught one that failing, testing things, improvising is essential to learning. *Results* provided feedback. Regrettably, I can still savor the pepper I'd poured into those first cookies.

Surely, it's healthy to realize early that setbacks are simply lessons, not moral judgments. I also discovered early that it's right and proper (as psychologist Abraham Maslow taught) to step back after we fail, to rest and reflect on the matter, to lick our wounds, sort things out, and only then grow again. That goes into the *true* learning that shows us *how* to learn, build competence and courage for the life we're uniquely created to live.

Little wonder that when I became a teacher, such issues were of the greatest significance. I quickly specialized in individualized instruction—the only sensible way to teach and learn. All my life, I've been moved to foster the type of hope and courage that my various teachers fostered in me. Especially when we falter or feel afraid, it can help so much to hear someone else say (even a character in a book), "I've found things do get better if we just have a little faith."

Exercise was a vital part of Madame's regimine. Each morning, rain or shine, well before 6 am, we two went for a *long*, brisk walk, war or no. I still walk daily, but not that early.

We children were expected to fit into an adult world. Part of that was knowing when to speak up about our experiences of, say, school or friends, and when to keep still. Mostly we chose the latter.

YOUTH'S INNER WITNESS

My move toward solitary study, reading, pondering along a line of private thought was inborn. Over a lifetime, good friends have understood. Back then, not so much. I was expected to be sociable—a nuisance to me.

People were immensely enjoyable, but something else more so.

Unlike a young Jesus, I lacked words and courage to say that I was being about "my Father's business." So I kept that pleasure to myself. Before age five, I craved time to think and read or simply play alone while experiencing the most luminous subjective realms. My mother and I occasionally sat quietly, reading alongside each other. That was rare. Only my grandmother spoke of "the religious impulse" as something highly desirable. I still thank God for her.

With her or Madame, a wordless companionship ensued. Both women were atypically self-contained; each enjoyed her own company as much as I did mine. In Shanghai, my mother was effervescent, social, very outgoing. She assumed I'd be entertaining, politely accommodating—like her. In my "false" self, I complied.

CONTRADICTIONS

Compared to Mémère or Madame, my mom increasingly hovered. Which I hated. I admired her so much. Yet, to her dismay, I recoiled from her clinging. That felt suffocating.

I was supposed to be decorous, submissive, pleasing to others—as my mother was raised to be. Was I also expected to be unduly obedient with parents and later with a husband? If so, I failed. I *did* want to please my parents; I *was* polite, but never passive. The older and more autonomous I got, the more upset with that self-rule my mom became. In my teens, she'd complain, "I gave you too

much freedom." Opposing pulls: In my own being I felt glad, yet also guilty for thwarting my mother's agenda: To raise a docile daughter who'd surpass tradition—as a gracious hostess, homemaker and grateful attendant to her mother. That daughter did not exist.

As a hostage to her own ghosts, my mother lived in her past. When distraught, she seemed furious about something ever unnamed. At her best, my mom was tender, caring, protective. Increasingly, however, she grew preoccupied, uninvolved in so much that concerned Anthony or me. Her "mother love" felt needy. She wanted *our* care, companionship, guardianship. For instance, she did not (could not?) attend to what her children were learning, at least not in any insightful, substantive way.

Had she not noticed that Mémère and Madame's values were diametrically opposed to hers? They encouraged self-sufficiency; my mom fought against her own, hence feared my independence. Anthony was increasingly away with friends. That made me her source of comfort. Our love for each other was enduring, but seemed of a non-verbal nature. No deep conversational rapport existed. As the interior Light increased, an unseen spiritual world opened. And with that the gulf widened between us. Before long, the inner "prompt" to do this or that made my own judgment matter more than anyone's; I rejected anything that opposed the freedom of what felt like a predestinated life. Until my thirties, I lacked words for this. Even now such matters are difficult to express.

Did my mom realize that Madame believed in giving a child plenty of time to concentrate, to shape her own development? Before a day's lessons she'd say, "The mind can be taught to stay with an idea or project. You train it. Don't let your thoughts lead you astray." Fortunately, if interested in something, I did not like being interrupted. What a luxury to read, to draw, to think or to ride horses on my own, or to laze about on warm grass watching cloud creatures roll by.

When my mother was feeling confident, she too loved her own thoughts, and disliked being pestered. If I complained of feeling bored, she'd say, "*Amusez vous.*"[21] That bracing dictum taught me to interest myself.

IN A STRANGE LAND

The preference for solitude inevitably became a source of friction between us: I liked to focus on things for long

---

21. Amuse yourself

22

stretches of time. She wanted my company—especially when my father was away.

Anthony and my mom seemed kindred spirits. They chit-chatted frequently about fashion, hair styles, people. My social pleasures ran to exchanges that drew out ideas and insights from all parties. I don't say it's "better," just different. Craving the affinity born of genuine intimacy, I suppose I longed for the meeting of spiritual minds.

When, in my twenties, I reflected on a youthful Jesus chiding his own parents for interrupting him, I realized my life's core conflict:[22] Namely, an inherent way of being that, if honored, easily leads to others' discomfort.

Consider the young, saintly Theobaldus who ran off to a monastery without his parents' permission. When his crying father begged the lad to come home, he scolded his elder. "Sir," the boy said, "Don't upset me. Leave me in peace and go in peace." [23] It's an uncommon friend, spouse, or parent who means it when saying, "Be and do whatever brings you joy." How I wish I'd had the nerve to say, "Don't upset me. Go in peace." when my parent fretted about my preference for solitude.

My grandmother understood. Loving the prophet Isaiah, she'd say, "Heed the silent nudge—that tells you, 'Go to the left. Go to the right.'"[24] Of course, although I did heed that voice, I felt badly about shrugging off my mother's attentions—as if I had to apologize for being solitary and studious. Had I been a boy, would a reflective

---

22. Luke 2:49—"I must remain in my Father's house."
23. D. Weinstein, R. Bell, *Saints in Society,* (Chicago/London: University of Chicago Press, 1992), 59. (Paraphrased quote)
24. Isaiah 30:21

disposition been as troubling? Years passed before accepting myself "as is."

There was decided pressure (spoken and unspoken) to conform to the stereotypical role my mom felt herself obliged to play; which was odd, since in many respects she was totally original, and defended others' emotional experience. I believe her symptoms of, say, loneliness, later, depression and worse, spoke out in the language of her buried self, all that she'd denied. Lacking an authentic outlet, her most exquisite nature eventually revealed itself as illness.

I, too, had an unwillingness, or inability to articulate certain vibrant realities. Some Transcendentalist summed this up: "When I try to speak of the Infinite, my tongue grows dumb on its hinges."[25] No dogma or congregational affiliation has helped; I felt, still do, "an exile in a strange land," as Psalm 137:4 frames it. Which of course relates to the alienation that is, as Jesus taught, a *positive* sign: If we were of this world, the world would love us. We know we are God's children, not offspring of the darkness, by that sense of being outsiders.

Which may explain why books—and more—the *ideas* and various characters in my favorite stories helped to untangle such knots.

"I'LL ALWAYS SAY MY PRAYERS..."

Beauty and the Beast, Heidi, Lassie, Black Beauty were among books I reread endlessly. The empathy for horses—what elsewhere I've called simple goodness—that radiated from Anna Sewell's *Black Beauty* mirrored Sewell's own suffering, as well as the goodness I experienced in our home.

---

25. It was either Walt Whitman or Emerson, and I've probably mangled the statement.

In particular, *Heidi's* uncomplicated faith, her relationship with her grandfather, the twists and turns of her
young life let me feel less fearful, less different. *Heidi*
amplified my love for the elderly (given Mémère's presence
and friendship in my life). Having lost her parents, Heidi's
plight made her story my own. Since my father was gone
and my mother's mothering had diminished, *Heidi* was the
right book at the right time.

Heidi's prayer life bolstered mine. Her faith that things
would work out, that with patience, God's plans for us
would unfold, eventually matched my sentiments. *Heidi*
was a comfort: "I'll always say my prayers..." she said,
trusting that even if God doesn't answer us immediately, all
would be well in due course. I didn't know it then, but
author Johanna Spyri's strengthening words of faith watered
the seeds of faith that early prayers and reflective reading
had planted. The result, as I grew, was a guidance and safe
passage through the dark journey that was to come.

Time to read, think, draw, or horseback ride quick-
ened my sense of aliveness, as if in steady Companionship.
That Presence prompted intense prayers, especially at
night. At such times, it seemed a beneficent God had
poured light into my being. Giving myself over to prayer, I
felt vital, confident, able to be and do more.[26] What good
fortune that no adult during those first years was ultra-
authoritarian. What pressure I felt was subtle. Left free to
daydream, I imagined impossibilities.

Books about God—or spiritual topics, or animals,
where good triumphs over evil —held my attention like no
others. Over time, comic books (never as schoolwork)—

---

26. For an invigorating discussion of this idea, see: Alice Miller, M.D., *The Drama of the Gifted Child*, (New York: Basic Books, 1989).

such as *Little Lulu, Nancy and Sluggo, Archie,* and the superheroes: *Superman, Batman, Captain America, Wonder Woman* among others—played a central role in the Americanization of yours truly. Even though he was away, my dad's openness to popular culture shaped my tastes in music, reading, ideas.

My father had "soul."[27] One saw in him a whole gamut of human feeling—pain, amusement, affection. He loved jazz, soul music, pop culture, philosophy and cartoons. *The Shmoos,* Al Capp's perfect, playful comic-strip creatures, had a place in our home. Shmoos made perfect playmates for children. Sadly, their days were numbered because they were delicious to eat.

My mother, somewhat of a highbrow, never read a comic, comic-strip, or pop fiction novel. Opera was her love. She had a purist's heart, a rather stylized, aesthetic sense— as in Japan or Italy's high culture.

On the other hand, as a card-carrying romantic, movies, later television, Broadway plays, captivated my mom. She said she saw (while pregnant with me) *Gone with the Wind* several times. We all thought she looked like Scarlett O'Hara, with whose character I suspect she identified.

AN ARTIST'S SENSIBILITY

My mother beautified our home, no matter where we lived. She sought out good taste in fashion, home decor, grooming, posture, tone of voice, and above all manners.

---

27. *The Urban Dictionary* defines "soul", in part, as when someone likes to think deeply, strangely, and (to paraphrase) who likes to be alone to consider the mysteries of the world cosmos, etc. And I mean it in the street sense of having deep, complex emotions, related to the nuances of human expression in art, music, sensuality, and the entire range and complexity of human feeling, regardless of culture.

My theatrical mother loved everything about the Japanese aesthetic.

Her's was a near visceral response to anything crude or low. She'd casually toss flowers into a vase, with exquisite results. Her intuitive "read" of people, wherein she simply knew their worries or vulnerabilities, enabled her to caution us beforehand: "Don't mention his wife's illness;" "Don't stare at the scar on her hand." We were taught to shield others from pain or embarrassment. My mom noticed who wanted what at meals, then tenderheartedly gave up something she craved so that another might have it. (Years later, when money was tight for us both, we'd send each other a hundred dollars to buy something special. The hundred just kept circulating back and forth between us; we wanted the other to have it.)

Both my mother and grandmother were extraordinarily empathic. Endless little talks, object lessons, marked my education about what, today, we'd call boundaries. Such empathy was second -nature to the women in our home. They *noticed* everything, but protected others from what they saw. Although we had servants, Anthony and I cleaned our own rooms. The rule was: Respect everyone, regardless of position or function. Tone of voice mattered as much as what was said.

Mémère framed such obligations in terms of moral elevation—"because it's good and right." My mother observed attitude: "*Who* do you think you're speaking to?" she'd demand if one's voice sounded the least bit rude. The grown-ups modeled consideration so there was no confusion about how Anthony and I were to behave.

Meals presented an ideal time for tutorials in expected etiquette: Lovely ways mirrored my mother's underlying aesthetic. To her, an elegant manner reflected God's touch. Beauty seemed her gateway to spirituality, although I never heard her speak of such things. She never mentioned God.

"THE LITTLE ROUNDED KNIFE IS FOR BUTTER ."

My mom patiently coached us on anything related to behavior or appearance: "Put your napkin on your lap when you sit down to a meal." "When you're done, fold it neatly and place it to the left of your plate." "Wait until everyone is served before you start eating.", "Finish what you're chewing, and swallow it, before speaking.", "Use the soup spoon and scoop soup *away* from you; sip it quietly.", "The little fork with three prongs is for fish, and the little rounded knife is for butter."

In later childhood, if I joined my parents at a hotel or restaurant for meals, my mother watched closely to ensure that I'd absorbed her instructions. Still later, when meeting a beaux's parents for dinner, or dining at some corporate event, I'd silently give my mom a nod of thanks.

"IF THE COAT FITS, WEAR IT, BUT KEEP MUM ABOUT VISIONS."

Aunt Jeanne (my mother's oldest sister, now in California), sent me a navy-blue, boiled-wool coat for Christmas. For a four year old, its itchy, heavy fabric was unbearable. Fashionable? Yes. So my mother reasoned that if I wore it, I'd please my aunt. How could someone in L.A. *see* what someone in China was wearing? My mom insisted. I wore it. The back of my neck broke out in a red rash from constantly scratching at the collar. Apparently style trumped comfort. This bit, I never quite grasped.

My first bedroom looked like a ballet studio: Airy and graceful; spacious, a bit austere. Saintly types could have worshiped there, contemplatives could have prayed. Which I did, from my earliest age. Some rooms, like that one, are simply good for children, and make them glad.

The room housed two of us—Madame and me. There were two of everything (dressers, bookshelves, desks), and two single beds, one at each end of the room, with a wide empty space in-between. Books were neatly stacked: on the floor, window sills, by the beds. The bookcases were filled. If, today, it sounds odd to think of a child and her governess sharing one room, for me, it was a comfort.

With Madame on guard, I felt safer, even with air raids and bombing, than ever I did for years thereafter in peacetime. As I'll explain, the spirit of fear arrived only *after* the War.

One night—at the foot of my bed—I saw an angelic presence sitting, just watching. It was no dream. I told three people.

Mémère said something like, "God gives us each a guardian angel. Little children, still so close to the other side, sometimes see theirs. Yours is protecting you, and always will." What a darling grandmother! She always dignified my confidences. Her advice lingers: "Heed your inside, silent voice that tells you, 'Go this way, not that,' [28] and "Marshinka, God has put His House, His eternity, into your heart."[29] I did sense God *with* me, and was aware of what, today, a friend calls, "Heaven's inaudible hum." Energetically speaking, that "hum" feels like the agapé love, ever-present. as Emmanuel, God with us.

When I told my mom about my vision, she made a *tsk* sound, and said, "You were dreaming." Madame listened seriously, fixed her clear blue eyes on mine, and nodded, "Maybe such things we keep to ourselves, yes?" So came a first tutorial in private versus public realities. Many such lessons followed, and I began to conceal (not curb) my spiritual intensity.

LESSONS AND CONTEMPLATIVE INFLUENCES

Benedictine mystic Hildegard of Bingen, believed that religious intensity is weakened only by indifference.[30]

---

28. Isaiah 39:21
29. Ecclesiastes 3:11
30. Fiona Bowie, *The Wisdom of Hildegard of Bingen* (Grand Rapids, MI: Eerdemans, 1997).

Never indifferent, my intensity went underground. Some say another name for the devil is *"the hinderer."* My hindrance was wanting to please, deciding early to guard my privacy in matters religious so as not to upset anyone. At the time, it made sense. It was a mixed bag: Fruitful in that I avoided hearing lectures or negativity about my interior life. Unfruitful in that for too long I didn't express my love of God. That ardor was unwelcomed conversation.

My grandmother and governess were exemplary models of the quiet self-governance that assures privacy. No one invaded either's space. My ever-gracious mother was inordinately polite, and accommodating. I waffled back and forth between these contraries. In school, I emulated my grandmother and Madame. No teacher could force me to say or do what went against conscience. It shocks me still that such trouble didn't faze me. I *cared* about angering those in authority, but didn't budge. Yet, with my parents, I was ever wanting to please. Not until adulthood (way past college) did I cease feeling guilty about choosing what I preferred. The tag "selfish," hounded me.

Growing up in a circle that discouraged "God-talk" forced me to invent ways to be understood. My humor, relational skills, and spirituality seemed all-of-a-piece, geared to infinite variety.

Of late, I speak my mind as is appropriate, decline invitations without feeling blameworthy, or giving excuses. In terms of "how to" shape my kind of life, this is foundational. No one is contemplative—even in a monastery—who is ambivalent, or lacks time for prayer, meditation, thoughtful study. (Merton wrote that the "active livers" in a contemplative setting hinder those truly called to that life.) In childhood, that heart posture surfaced as a spontaneous love of my own company. Except when something enchanting was offered in the outer sphere. Like my mother's cooking lessons.

THE KINGS' PUDDING AND OTHER GOODIES

During the War, we children were largely unaware of rationing. We didn't miss meals, no doubt due to the chickens and other animals that were raised for us. Our entire household had the essentials.

A mandatory beverage at all meals was goat's milk, boiled for health reasons. Each cup, having been scalded, had a disgusting layer of skin on top. Once that film was removed, the milk was perfectly fine.

Another treat came when my mom taught Anthony and me about cooking. She'd narrate the how-to of a dish while she made, say, what she called, "the pudding of Italian kings"—a simple, sublime, dessert.

After beating raw egg yolks and sugar until these became a pale yellow, thread-like custard,[31] she'd daintily pour the mixture into egg cups. I loved those little bone china cups, translucent with tiny yellow buttercups painted around the top. My mom said, "Make beauty a part of the meal." The dessert was delicious. What with goat's milk and the freshest of eggs, we grew up healthy, loving to cook, and to eat and to entertain with a flourish.

Less often, we'd all walk into a nearby commercial area to an ice cream parlor called The Chocolate Shoppe. A little bell rang cheerily when we opened the door to

---

31. It turns out this was *zabaglione,* prepared without the Marsala wine—the latter being a standard ingredient in the traditional dessert. Today for safety's sake, one avoids raw eggs.) Not so, back then; particularly when hens are raised in clean, humane, free-range settings.

delectable scents of vanilla and chocolate. We were giddy with delight; ice cream during the War was rare.

Cooking lessons, ice cream treats, relaxed discussions as we walked to and from The Chocolate Shoppe were some of the sunniest times any child could have. But the warmest time of all was when my father returned.

EUPHORIC HOMECOMING

Father and son at a picnic – right before my dad's P.O.W. days.

Thankfully, when the War ended, the Americans freed all the prisoners and my dad and he returned in one piece. Seeing him was at once a thrill and a heartache. Frail, stick-thin; the man who walked through our front door was not the jovial, robust one who had left. Many captives were not so fortunate.

From about 1939 to the War's end in 1945, the Japanese Army imprisoned over 140,000 of those associated with the Allied military forces, selected community leaders—either citizens of the Allied nations and/or business heads. My dad's association with Chinese industrialists must have made him a prime candidate for the Japanese camps.

Thousands of those imprisoned were transported to Japan's mainland to work in construction, road and railroad-building jobs, or sent elsewhere to replace Japan's depleted workforce. By the time the War was over, more than *30,000* had died (within and outside Japan's mainland) from starvation, disease, and/or horrific mistreatment.[32] I cannot bear to go into this.

The camps were brutal; perhaps barbaric in spots. Was my father's life spared because he spoke a bit of Japanese, had deep knowledge—and sincere fondness—for Japan, its people, its culture? He may have suffered. I'll never know. My father would not speak of his ordeal.

None of us knew what he'd undergone, or what atrocities he'd seen. He rebounded, but thereafter experienced bouts of the malaria that he'd contracted while imprisoned. He never uttered a word against the Japanese. The slur "Jap" or any other racial insult was unthinkable in our home. Quite literally: We did not *think* that way; such ideas never entered the mind. We were just not that type of family.

---

32. www.forces-war-record.com.uk/Prisoners of War, Japanese 1939-1945.

"DON'T LOOK BACK."

Family and friends on our last day in Shanghai.

Despite the trauma of war, the memory of those years in China burns bright and happy. That household of disparate people was family. Even so, as soon as the War ended, my father moved us to America. With that, our close-knit group unraveled: Mèmère went to live with her other son (my Uncle Roger) who also left China. We hugged and kissed goodbye, and my grandmother whispered, "Don't look back. God is Emmanuel—right here, *with* you, right now—don't ever look back."[33] My grandmother was wise. She and I corresponded, but didn't see one another again

---

33. Mémère must have been referring to Genesis 19:26: Lot's wife was turned into a pillar of salt and died, because she turned her attention back to focus on all she loved and valued, instead of moving forward with Life's plan and purposes.

until I was a young woman. Childhood's love endured. Yet we had changed. She had her new, very active life; I had mine. She's gone now, but is still in my prayers.

Madame found another position. We never saw each other or corresponded. My Uncle Albert went to California, where we continued to see each other until his death a decade or so later. Our household help went their separate ways. Such bonds, such closeness—then poof: Gone.

The initial excitement of finally going to America blunted the obvious: We were leaving Shanghai. In time, I felt the ache of that first separation from family. "Don't look back" is easier said than done.

Soon after we left, I experienced a more profound loss: Through my first five years, I'd known the love of three caring mothers: Mémère, Madame, and my mom. Two of the three were now gone. I never imagined my mother leaving, too.

On the day we flew to America, my final farewell was to my horse.

ೋ

PART II

COMING TO AMERICA

My parents with Aunt Jeanne and Uncle Jack at a nightclub.

Chapter 3

HOME OF THE BRAVE

...there is a [temperament] that characterizes artists—
impatience, fear of being trapped in stable situations, an
unwillingness to be led...an arrogant belief in one's own
authority —**Ben Shahn**[34]

Picture 1946: Everyone is jubilant that World War II has ended. My parents, Anthony, and I head for America. My dad looks ashen and tired, but relieved—eager to get back to the States. My mom, who loves travel, is her old self, radiant, happy to be flying away.

Air travel, like going to dentists, was painful back then. A mixed odor of gasoline fumes, synthetic fabrics, and the vapors of disinfectants greeted all who entered the cabin. One whiff, even before takeoff, was bad enough to make one retch. (Especially *this* one.)

In the decade or so after the War, commercial airliners were often converted cargo or military planes: Fat bodied, clunky—rattling throughout a flight. This may have been the trip when my father spotted a famous woman in our cabin. Rising from his seat, he told me, "Don't look now, but there's someone I admire on board." The signature on the autograph he acquired for me read: "Eleanor Roosevelt."

---

34. Ben Shahn, John D. Morse, ed., *Ben Shahn,* (New York: Praeger Publishers, 1972), 198.

We stopped over in Hawaii for a week. I'd never experienced breezes so soft and fragrant; colors so vivid. Everything was new to me. Honolulu's white sandy beaches were enticing. For one who had never swum in the ocean, that blue, glass-like stillness was deceptive. Without warning, a strong current pulled me into deeper waters. I nearly drowned. I told no one. My near miss with death in the deep blue, and a painful, blistering red sunburn, caused a dislike of the beach ever after.

Our first sighting of the U.S. was emotional.[35] To this day, I get choked up when hearing Neil Diamond's song, *Coming to America.* Who wouldn't relive the feelings of long, high expectation, and then thankfulness of finally reaching what is seen as a Promised Land?

New York was our home base, but we paused for a week in California. We visited my Aunt Jeanne (my mother's older sister—she of the dreaded boiled-wool coat), her husband—my Uncle Jack, and Uncle Albert. Various cousins on my mother's side also lived in Los Angeles. They all came to see us, with what seemed a lot of tears and hugging.

We crowded into my aunt and uncle's home in Sherman Oaks. Every structure in L.A. seemed jammed up against the next. I'd never seen a tract house before. How baffling to find looming over that miniscule lot, in watery blueness, a huge swimming pool. Artist David Hockney's iconic pool series brings back that California image with nostalgic, aqua clarity.

There was no garden, hardly any vegetation, just shimmering aqua water bordered by pinkish cement, and

---

35. Hawaii, although a U.S territory, did not qualify as a State yet. It didn't become our 50th state until August 21, 1959 under President Dwight Eisenhower.

a few straggly green ferns. Jeanne and Jack had a darling, silky-smooth, very affectionate dachshund. A house-man arrived daily—which I thought odd considering the tiny residence. He did just about everything, except cook. That was my aunt's secured domain.

Aunt Jeanne rarely left home from what I could tell. She'd drive to the market, to a few relatives who lived in Beverly Hills, and back again. Her life centered around the immediate family, relatives, and household affairs.

Aunt Jeanne was a fastidious homemaker whose house smelled like freshly-cut lemons. She used lemons for nearly everything. She'd slice lemons in half for cooking, squeeze the juice into salads or savory dishes, then plop the used halves into a pan of soapy hot water that held cooking utensils and dishes in a sort of wash-as-you-go fashion. After a meal, more lemons went into cleaning up; she'd scour the sink with the rinds, and polish the bottoms and insides of pans with them. Her sink, pots, plates sparkled.

Uncle Jack was a realtor who specialized in desert land—Palm Desert, I think, and perhaps new developments where hundreds of homes looked like cartoon copies of each other.

Uncle Albert lived in the city. He didn't drive due to a continual neck spasm, but visited us nearly every day. He rode a bus for hours to get from his apartment to my aunt and uncle's. Always in good spirits, Albert had been hurt in the War so that his neck was permanently askew and shaking. Or, he'd been born that way. None of that mattered to any of us. Of all my mother's relations, Albert was the one I loved most. I never really warmed up to the others; it's entirely possible that they hadn't really warmed up to me. A studious girl who shuns small talk is not the most

My Uncle Albert at his restaurant job.

captivating company. I was simply unwilling to join in what seemed pointless banter, or be led astray from my own thoughts. A cousin once described me to another (within Anthony's earshot), "She's pale, but interesting, don't you think?" Thereafter, when in good spirits, my brother would address me, "Hey, pale and interesting."

KEBABS, RED SOCKS AND A GRAY SILK KIMONO

Aunt Jeanne, also born in Cairo, was an accomplished, generous cook. Without asking if we were hungry, she'd pile our plates high with her savory Middle Eastern fare: Shashlik (lamb kebabs), falafel, tabbouleh, and her mix of European and Eastern dishes. Jeanne was the most Americanized of the three sisters (my mother, my Aunt Alys, and Jeanne). Only she could drive. Her car of choice was a long, white, four-door Cadillac. As she was so petite, drivers of cars beside hers must have had a fright since the top of her head didn't quite reach the top of the steering wheel. She could see out, but it looked as though no one was driving—an impossibility in the fifties.

I think Uncle Jack was a Syrian-American, extremely successful in real estate (so we were told), and he rarely spoke. Maybe he just didn't speak to me. Anyway, like Jeanne, Jack was exceedingly short—not quite five feet tall. The two were well matched—rather like bookends. Aunt Jeanne was strong minded, somewhat tough, quite dominant. She must have worked hard to hold her own, surrounded as she was by three men who, one imagines, held many Middle Eastern views about male authority at home.

Uncle Jack always wore red socks (even, years later, to my wedding). Whenever I saw him—and my visits spanned a decade or so—Jack was lounging around the house in a calf-high, gray silk kimono, anklet type, red socks, and slippers. Did he wear anything under his kimono? Thankfully, he kept it closed— tied at the waist with its sash, and he didn't move around much. He reclined on his couch throughout the day (every day that I saw him) drinking Scotch or something brown and alcoholic, while listening to news on a complex pre-and-post War radio called a Hallicrafter.

Uncle Jack was kind. Yet his ideas about many things, probably including gender issues, were outdated. What I viewed as the "alcoholic haze" in which Jack lived may not have been the only reason he and I never got to know one another. He and Jeanne were complicated, difficult for me to talk to, so I quickly learned to keep my distance. I'd been taught to be polite to my elders. Keeping quiet in their presence and putting a decent bit of space between us seemed the wisest choice. Even so, a familial love of sorts developed. So odd how affection grows between people who have absolutely nothing to say to each other.

Jack and Jeanne had two sons close in age. The younger one introduced me to bubble gum with a box of one hundred Double Bubble gum pieces. Each pink square was individually wrapped in little wax paper cartoon strips. I couldn't get enough.

My mother warned me not to chew gum before bed. I ignored her, fell asleep with a wad of it in my mouth. Which ended up in my hair and had to be cut out. Viewed through the eyes of experience, my affinity for those cousins changed over time. They were good to my mother; for me that friendship cooled. This seems a norm in family relations. Or, perhaps that's primarily true of my family.

A HOME NEAR CENTRAL PARK

After California, we flew on to New York, taking up residence for several months in a spacious hotel suite near Park Avenue. A friend who lives in Greenwich Village to whom I've described it, thinks the hotel may have been the Essex House or the Stanhope, both near Central Park where I rode almost daily.

Anthony sometimes rode with me but I liked, perhaps preferred, to ride by myself. At least back then, riding through that park lent itself to the enjoyments of reflection. Not that a child thinks in those terms but the lack of distracted small talk, the aloneness, the sheer ineffable loveliness of trees, grasses, bird songs gave rise to the sort of satisfaction unavailable in normal day-to-day life with others. I was not a "God-seeker." Maybe I was a "God-responder" having apprehended a call to which I felt obliged to listen; and to reply. That sense was (still is) amplified by natural beauty. I was getting old enough to revel in these contemplative experiences. Surely these moments led to my adulthood's love of driving, alone on long trips.

When designed, over 150 years ago, Central Park may have been planned to be experienced from horseback. The bridle paths in the park wind through lush, well-manicured grounds, and there are miles of these paths amidst some 900 plus acres of trees, open spaces, and thriving vegetation. For a child as interior as I was, the setting made for a spectacular, rural feeling right in the heart of the city.

Long-distance runners must understand: Such times are unsurpassed for creative thought, planning, and introspection. These "ultimate athletes," to borrow author George Leonard's phrase, experience the slow-down of time, the heightened perception and lucidity that accompany extreme sports. Of course, running can be a meditation that sharpens awareness.[36]

OUR JAZZY NEW YORK DAYS

My dad, the consummate urbanite, felt at home in New York. He'd lived there as a boy. Now, preoccupied with rebuilding most, if not all, of his former exporting enterprise, he seemed fully engaged. My mother was "herself" again. She adored New York, had friends there, luxuriated in the shops, the night life, and the theater. She and my father led what seemed, to Anthony and me, a charmed life.

---

36. Please check out *Creative Rest,* a conversation with J. Rossini about the innovative potentials of extreme sports and thought tactics of highly inventive sorts: Marsha Sinetar, A Casual Contemplative's Archive, YouTube.

Through the early 1950s, my parents were a popular couple. Their friends were what I'd term "beautiful people."

My mother's best friend, Zazi, was one of those women you'd never forget. An interpreter for the United Nations, Zazi's job and fashion flair epitomized cosmopolitan life. Tall, slim, animated, the Swiss-French Zazi was surprisingly single. That intrigued me. I was already aware that single women were unusual. However alluring, women such as these were not to be emulated by me. The interesting thing was that no one ever diminished or marginalized her, perhaps because she was so buoyant, so effervescent. She fairly oozed an upbeat confidence.

The highly intelligent Zazi had an enviable career, no children, and seemed superbly self-reliant. Both my mother and father respected her. I also noticed my dad conversed with her about the news, politics, foreign affairs in a more serious manner than with other women. A new lesson that, at six or so, demanded deliberation.

Zazi and my mom were polar opposites. Was Zazi's freedom something my mother coveted? Would she have had the temerity to pursue a single life? More lessons. What child isn't schooled by such wonderings?

It's likely many young girls of my generation (though not yet the majority) sensed the inequity of female roles and opportunities. Mine was the era of girls who suppressed ideas of what life might be for them—ideas most unlike that of their mothers. Most of us sensed what we wanted, but may have vicariously fulfilled these dreams through others, for example our husbands. Certainly, I was being groomed for that traditional role. Surely, that was not my call. No wonder that Zazi's example made a lasting impression. As had Madame and Mémère. With my first step into America, I began patching together ideas of what life at its best could be.

After reading my book, *The Mentor's Spirit*, the female president of a recording company told me, "I, too, as a child, began storing up a patch-work quilt of images from which I created my own kind of life."

Equally instructive were my parents' soireés. I'd watch my elegant mother dress for a cocktail party as she described the ins and outs of applying makeup. I'd sprawl on the floor, while she narrated how to brush hair so that a dress didn't get soiled, and what to wear so as to always be appropriate. Her secret, learned in the convent: "You'll always be well dressed in a navy blue or black suit and a beautifully tailored, white silk blouse." Mother knows best. That was my costume of choice in my corporate practice.

THE PLAY'S THE THING

Whether there were actors and actresses present at my parents' gatherings, I can't say. However, all the adults looked glamorous and quite theatrical.

To watch *The Thin Man* film series starring William Powell and Myrna Loy as Nick and Nora Charles, is to understand my parents' social persona. Attitudes, stylishness seemed of a type. For example, both my mom and Nora Charles were sleek, and gregarious. Nick Charles smoked, drank, played the ponies and he was witty. That was my dad, whose dry humor was quietly perceptive. He also drank, smoked, gambled. There the similarities end. My father—erudite, serious, highly principled—never played the fool, which Nick's character perfected as an art form. My father didn't have "shtick."

My parents' fashionable friends weren't all rich. They seemed on the fringe of what then was called "café society"—people who frequented night clubs, the best plays and restaurants, and stayed current on popular books and ideas.

Anthony and I were required to make an appearance at these functions. We paraded around, conversed politely with guests, then were whisked away by a nanny. It felt scripted. One was applauded if clever, attractive, and above all, *adaptable*—able to play one's part as each guest demanded. It was improv—live theater, where one stayed in character. Or shifted on a dime. That meant rising to the occasion of the smart, impromptu banter at hand. Invigorating as these performances were, a few moments of frivolous talk was tiresome. Anthony, the born actor, could ham it up. He amused everyone, and flourished in a party climate. I always wondered why he hadn't chosen a stage career.

I held my own, but was shy—ever more so as I grew into the self-consciousness of adolescence. Still, these festivities were educational. We were watching those who'd mastered the art of social nuance; indeed, we were surrounded by virtuosos.

Ours was a musical family. Anthony and I played piano and sang. In our teens, we were both good ballroom dancers. Anthony was an especially droll mimic. He'd purposely sing off-key, tricky to do intentionally. He expertly imitated Broadway singer Ethel Merman and crooner Johnny Mathis. For instance, he'd sing *White Christmas,* hilariously going flat on the last notes of each verse. To make me laugh, in crowded hotel elevators, he'd hum (loudly) off-pitch, as if unaware.

Both my parents loved music and, party or not, there was plenty of it wafting through our home: for my dad. jazz pianists Fats Waller, Oscar Peterson, and George Shearing, singers Billie Holliday, and Nat King Cole; for my mother, French singer Edith Piaf, Broadway tunes, and Italian opera. New York's normalcy was full of pizazz.

Liberation came when my parents left for an evening out. I'd fix myself two bologna sandwiches on Wonder Bread (with lots of lettuce and mayo), hop onto the middle of the bed, and listen to the radio: *The Shadow; I Love a Mystery; Alfred Hitchcock; Burns and Allen*—it was "The Golden Age of Radio." Radio was our minds' playground, so whenever possible the whole family gathered around agreeably.

If *Jack Benny* or *Burns and Allen* were on, my dad—if near—would draw close. The sound of his deep chuckling made me happy. My mother favored opera. If *Madame Butterfly* or *Pagliacci* were featured, she'd sing along (dramatically, piercingly, with lots of vibrato) which infuriated me—particularly if reading. I'd scowl at her, take up my books, and huff out of the room. She'd laugh and sing louder.

HIGH CULTURE AND CHEESEBURGERS

Manhattan offered *everything*. As did my dad. Which could explain why my mother's emotional balance returned when he was near. I'm only guessing that his presence, his success, his extravagance bolstered her sense of security. I think she felt safe, protected, pampered around him. So did I. To this day, I can't explain how he managed to rebound so successfully after his prisoner-of-war experience. He thought deeply and incessantly about life, about paradox and ideas like justice, mercy, forgiveness. Then, too, his love of what he did, the engagement and pleasures of work that he loved must have had a renewing effect. (No wonder I write of the restorative effects of a *much-loved* work or way of life). My dad's generous spirit seemed to be healing. He never gave sparingly.

One favored family story frames that portrait: It involved my father's present to my mom of a diamond ring. The jewelers, Van Cleef & Arpels, had wrapped the ring in a small, blue velvet gift box. Which my dad then hid in a gigantic, gold-foiled package, the size of a Volkswagen.

My mom dug through masses of snowy-white tissue paper to find the treasure. There were many stories like that, because when my dad had money, he spent it, and enjoyed indulging his wife. Anthony and I delighted in my parents' mutual affection, the warmth that must comfort any child. It was in that spirit of largess and liberality that my mother introduced me to New York's vibrancy.

That first spring marked our finest hours together while exploring the arts. My mother loved high culture and was an enthusiastic, civilizing tour guide. Her unrivaled refinement was inborn; she'd not been to college or finishing school. She simply "knew" what had value, flourishing in the atmosphere of museums, theater, and beautiful surroundings. Usually on Friday afternoons, we went to Carnegie Hall for concerts, musicals like *Annie Get Your Gun* and ballets, like Tchaikovsky's *Nutcracker*.

After such outings, we'd lunch or have tea at Schrafft's, a classic Manhattan restaurant. Early on, we tasted the deliciousness of cheeseburgers for the first time. After which, as the Lewis and Clark of burger joints, we sampled cheeseburgers all across the city. Years later in California when things weren't so grand, we continued our search for the tastiest burgers—the expedition provided a respite from our woes. So does sharing meals bring people together; whether at the kitchen table, the fanciest bistro, or hole-in-the-wall café.

We were all intuitive cooks. My mom, using no recipes, just her taste and imaginative recall of dishes, fixed us beef stroganoff, Chicken Kiev, or Crepe Suzettes as routinely as, say, other home cooks make tuna sandwiches or a meatloaf. Naturally, any excuse to dine out was a good one; what better city than Manhattan to try out restaurants?

When we went out for Chinese food—which we did frequently—my father ordered. Speaking in Cantonese or Mandarin, he'd request dishes usually not found on the menu. The waiters were all agog, fluttering around him excitedly, eagerly hoping to talk with my dad about their homeland—as if my dad were an old friend. For me, the scene was bitter-sweet; I wanted to cry for the sheer poignancy of the nostalgia that their obvious homesickness stirred in me. Those emotions linger today. It's likely many of us share that feeling (and, yes, even to the point of tears), if far from something or someone much loved. It's not usually a material loss. To paraphrase St. John Vianney, patron saint of parish priests, who apparently knew something about homesickness: "Here on earth we are like travelers, always living in hotels, yet longing for our true Home which is Heaven."

As a girl, ever wondering why I so often felt such longing for something obscure, I did not understand that born mystics (aka: contemplatives) rarely feel completely at home here. Over time, St. Augustine's precept clarified things: *God* is the soul's country—not this material dimension. Back then, it was a muddle.

Toward the end of that first summer in New York—with about a month to go— my mom began to change. Slowly, our museum-cheeseburger outings ended. My dad spoke of returning to the Near East by himself. My mom stayed in bed during the day. Once more, that vacant stare returned to her eyes. She was not with us. None of us knew what to do. If asked, she'd wave her hand nonchalantly as if shooing away a fly. Her routine reply? "*C'est rien.*"[37]

My dad's upcoming trip to India may have triggered her upset. Did she need my father's attendance to feel safe or stabilized? Did she lack the psychic strength to handle ordinary life on her own? She'd been trained to be a dutiful wife, a charming hostess, and conversationalist, with a husband always in charge. When she was well, she played those parts to perfection. When that script changed, havoc wrecked the scene.

In hindsight, it seems my mother lacked the skills and defenses for a *practical* effectiveness. Although bright, exquisitely tender, and highly polished, in some ways she was an innocent with no toughness. My mom gave indirect voice to a past problem, but could not actively speak of it or solve it in any workable, self-affirming way. Did that cause her to fury?

She was now preoccupied with some haunting memory. She expressed all that in wistful, regretful—albeit completely ambiguous—terms. What a drama; what a mystery.

Whatever the cause, the mother I loved was disappearing. Our family watched her coherence ebb-and-flow; her old self came in for a while, then, like the tide, went

---

37. "It's nothing."

out again. Anthony was away at a summer school. Initially, anxiety made me stick closer to her. That was new. Sensing myself a nuisance, I backed away, then clung more tightly. What to do? Nothing was said to make me uneasy, however the intuition was a forewarning.

Agitated by my mom's vacuity, I'd tug at her sleeve to pull her back from wherever she'd gone. After some moments of this, she'd abruptly get her mind into gear and, looking astonished, ask, "*Qu'est-ce que c'est?*[38] Why do you get so upset?" How does a child explain that she *senses* (more than she knows with her intellect) that something is very wrong?

To this day, when a gut-feeling warns of trouble, I pay attention. Is it "hyper-vigilance?" Or, as First Kings 19:11-14 puts it , is it that God is alive with us *as* our own internal cues? How fortunate that the painful trials of childhood can teach us to heed our silent cues.

In time, my mom's latent hostility emerged— it was rage. We all backed away. Despite her denials, I felt that my world was about to shift, but didn't know *how.* My clinginess may have frightened my mom, making matters worse for her. Once, during those weeks, my dad took me aside to say, "Your mother is having trouble with her nerves. We have to be patient." Anthony told me she was seeing a psychiatrist. In short order I was sent away— unexpectedly.

Summer camp: A totally alien concept to me—the last and worst place a bookish, introspective, now often anxious seven-year old wants to be. For all their sophistication, when it came to their children, my dear parents were clueless about what sparked dread. Possibly they couldn't

---

38. "What is it?"

afford to remember their own youthful fears. I know they had their share.

OLD-SCHOOL PARENTING. "SURPRISE!"

Suspecting (quite rightly) that I'd be upset, camp was kept secret. Until my parents dropped me off at a dismal, military-type structure, no mention was made of the plan. "Oh God, please no!" It was at the beach.

One July day, my father, mother, and I simply piled into a car, ostensibly to visit the New Jersey shore. We pulled into a gravel driveway, behind which sat an ugly set of cabins. My mom turned around to me from her front seat, and broke the news: Here was *"une occasion merveilleuse, mon petit cher"*[39]—my chance to be with other girls my age and enjoy the sun and the sea. Icy fear filled my being.

With fair, burn-instantly skin and my near-death episode in Hawaii, I was first scared, then outraged to be left somewhere detestable without warning or explanation. Didn't my parents know I *hated* the beach? What a nightmare. With fear, all thought of God disappeared.

AND THE OSCAR GOES TO...

Before my parents leave, a pear-shaped lady in olive-drab garb rushes out of the barracks, greets us all, and grabs my hand, which I promptly yank away. *Who* is this stranger and why is she touching me? Not one to make a scene, I now produce a prize winner. Those present viewed the following drama, undoubtedly worthy of an Academy Award.

---

39. "This is a marvelous opportunity, my little darling."

As a dark sedan pulls away from the curb, a frenzied commotion ensues. The car's adult occupants can be seen crying as a little blond girl running after it, tries to get back in. She is screaming, "Don't leave me, don't leave me..." The camp counselor chases the wailing child, yelling, "It'll be fine, you'll like it here." A gaggle of seven year olds, witnessing the hysteria, hold hands in a contagion of fear and anguish. They hug each other, and begin howling. The show continues through the night as the youngest inmates, huddled in bunk beds, cry themselves to sleep about their own internment. Yours truly sobs into her pillow, pleads to God to help her endure the unendurable.

A lifetime has passed, and I still wonder, "What were they thinking?" "Whose hot idea was that?" My parents may just as well have yelled, "Surprise! Here's something you'll hate."

The true surprise was that that experience did me good. It armed me with a resilience that I'd need in years to come.

FACING DOWN BULLIES

Need I add that the entire stay was hideous? Aside from my cell mates, who were fine, the place was visually offensive. And it smelled. Bed sheets, sinks and showers; floors, chairs and tables were sticky with sand or dirt. Or both. We ate mostly hot dogs and potato chips, and lumpy oatmeal for breakfast—all bland. There were no books, no writing supplies, no music at all save for the compulsory, exceedingly tedious singing of camp songs. All the girls my age were friendly. The older ones, in the undying practice of adults too busy or resistant to do their jobs, were put in charge of the younger ones. Herein the problem: The big girls were tyrants.

Daily, we were forced to drink in the delights of the sea. Two camp counselors drove us to the shore. They waited in the car, smoking and talking, while we supposedly swam. Hell is not fire; for me. it's the beach.

The older girls had a rule: We younger ones could not get back into the car if there was any sand on our feet. The unspoken threat? We'd be left behind.

No one had brought socks, so the moment we stepped into sandals to walk across the beach to the car, sand clung to our feet. The Catch-22 was obviously meant to torment us little captives.

I'd wash my feet in the ocean, wash off my sandals, then walk across sand. Another foot bath followed in an outdoor shower contraption, which again proved pointless. Fed-up with the game and so angry, I heard the small still voice inside say, "Just don't play."

Having heard about Gandhi's non-violent approach to British rule, a quiet resistance seemed right. So I went on strike, sat down on the sand, refusing to budge. Opposition was new to me, never wanting to defy my elders. What would the big girls do to me?

To my amazement, the older girls got confused, then nervous. They spoke of amending their rule. I stayed put, staring into space. Eventually, a camp counselor came out, calmly led me (sandy footed and all) to the car, glaring at the bullies, who looked sheepishly at their own feet. I should have remembered: I was in America now, and we don't tolerate tyranny. What a victory. What a lesson. There were no tears that night in the bunkhouse. I felt powerful. It paid to be tough in the Home of the Brave.

THE DEEPEST WOUND

By summer's end, my dad had enrolled Anthony in a military (boarding) school in upstate New York—Tarrytown, I think. It was a puzzle, sensitive and emotional as I was, that Anthony rarely showed his sadness. He didn't cry or carry on at the prospect of leaving us. I don't recall ever seeing him shed a tear, even when hugging us good-bye. (How like my father that seemed.) That brave young soldier buried his feelings deep down and headed out to battle.

Maybe, like me, he cried into his pillow at night. Or, like our dad, kept his emotions tightly controlled and under wraps. This seemed heroic since holding back tears is not something I do. Eventually, as emotional pain always does, his heartaches showed up, seeking release.

Tensions were brewing between my dad and brother; it seemed my father was especially hard on him. My dad rarely raised his voice with me—"the look" was enough. He was stern with Anthony, dissatisfied, annoyed. If my dad got angry with my brother, *I'd* cry, wanting peace between the two, longing to protect Anthony and see him in my dad's good graces. I sympathized, but how does a child protect an older sibling in the face of an all-powerful father? I never verbalized my impressions.

Whether the conflict was Anthony not tidying up his room or forgetting to do an assigned chore, somehow my brother's demeanor or work ethic grieved my dad. During these upsets, Anthony held on to his dignity, perhaps expressed his anger by undercutting—resisting—things my father valued. That pattern persisted.

By any measure, my parents held clear, stereotypical standards for their children: Boys fulfilled male roles; girls played their feminine parts.

My dad wanted something from Anthony that he simply could not deliver. Similarly, my mother expected me to be other than I was. Such disapprovals seem the most profound wound any parent can inflict on a child.

Years later, Anthony confirmed my suspicion—that my dad tried to "toughen" him up, to "make a man" out of him. Hence, the military school solution. From today's vantage point, that seems to have exacerbated the conflict between those two. Such choices were par for the parenting course in the old-school.

Anthony was an instinctive artist, highly aware of the subtlest nuances of others' looks and personality. Charm was his relational skill of choice. He was not scholastically inclined. Generally, he got on famously with my mother, who responded to his bitingly insightful critique of others and his fashion sense. Both had artistic taste in pretty much everything: Style, home decor, cuisine, architecture, entertainment, appearances. My socially precocious brother kept abreast of all manner of gossip about the adult world, so he and my mom were most compatible—as I was with my dad.

Anthony could be cruel one minute, captivating the next. If he wanted something, rather than asking straight out, he'd turn on the charm. In childhood, I looked the other way; later not so much.

LESSONS AND INFLUENCES

Life in the U.S. brought a mixed bag of emotions. I reconsidered my dad's leaving for prison camp at gunpoint, and imagined the worst about his experience, and considered my mother's decline. My grandmother and Madame's absence finally registered. Fear, sorrow, and anger crept in. Nameless anxiety co-existed with my natural exuberance. The latter, thankfully, outshone the former, but worry lingered. Some influences built confidence: my father's calming presence, my mother's love of us had a lasting, beneficent effect. Given the tensions between us, she'd be surprised to hear how her having brought such beauty and civility into our lives—what with those healing effects on the psyche—supported me over time. I credit that envelope of affection and graciousness for sealing our family in an enduring warmth. Music, the arts, the overarching aesthetic of our shared consciousness, added an optimism to my outlook that kept me going throughout darker times. (As a result, I've pondered why prisons or reform schools don't do more with the fine arts, most of which reflect the Light that is our most wholesome life.[40])

In New York, for instance, the helpful powers of beauty enabled my rebounding from being constantly separated from Anthony. And the trauma of being left at camp without warning. I learned that inner torments could be tolerated if a lavish interior life were present. Thankfully, a deepening experience of prayer increased my desire to grow in faith. In later decades, therapy revealed that early family affections also allowed hope to rise up *despite* grievous feelings. The "environment" factor cannot be denied, while developing a sturdy faith seems something else, entirely—something spiritually, consciously, steadily cultivated with one's daily choices. As the next vignette illustrates, the force of love (which

---

40. John 1: 4-5

flows *from* God, not persons[41]) also furthers faith. A contemplative (or mystic's) rule is that the inner shapes the outer. Truly, love, beauty, respect address a thousand wounds[42]. Any of us who've known such elements in childhood must sense that.

ONE UNFORGETTABLE CHRISTMAS

After the camp fiasco, my parents decided I'd travel with them for awhile. My mother was well; my father was optimistic; Anthony was home from school, looking grown-up and smart in his brass buttoned, gray wool uniform. On Christmas Eve, following a cozy dinner in our hotel, we had a party with my parents' friends, everyone happy and crowded about. The next day or so, Anthony and I toured shops. They were all decked out in gold, green and red trimmings. We'd not seen so many Santas before,standing on corners, ringing shiny brass bells, calling out, "Merry Christmas." The whole city celebrated the season. Twinkling lights, big red bows, shimmering tinsel—what child could forget the sight? Those few Manhattan days were idyllic. My mom was energized by my dad's presence, her cultural pursuits, friends, and New York's ambiance. My dad was thriving, expansive, enjoying his work. For me, that time represented "family life." The disruptions ahead never erased the gladness and closeness of that lovely brief time.

---

41. 1 John 4:19: We love, because God loves us *first*.

42. A dressing, we are told, comes in *direct contact* with a wound, thereby protecting it and furthering healing.

That December marked the coziest holiday we ever spent in America as a family. And the last. Its sustaining impression lifted my spirits in years to come. As did a growing intuitive practice of prayer. At seven years of age, I was still saying nightly prayers—blessing my family, petitioning God for this or that favor. A new sense of worship was forming: Wordlessly, there in my bed, the awareness of God that had always been with me, deepened. At times intuitively, I knew that I was *being* prayed more than actively

My father at a business meeting

praying. All I could do was sit in the stillness in awe and wonderment. Despite that burgeoning transcendence, I did not sense the extent of the dislocations to come.

We never had another Christmas like that in New York—never one where we were all together. My brother and I didn't see each other for the rest of our childhoods. Eventual reunion was caring, awkward. We'd grown apart, followed our own values and world-views. Each of us were led along unique—completely dissimilar—life paths. Over time, we visited less and less. At the deepest level we held on to that family feeling, but never again in quite the same way.

෧

Chapter 4

A TRAVELING SEASON

The soul, when it is really at peace with itself, is united to God.
—Julian of Norwich[43]

In New York, after Christmas, Anthony went to military school. From age seven through ten, non-stop travel was my norm. Between trips, while my dad evaluated political and business conditions in a country, I lived in boarding school. When we stayed put for a while, tutors came to our hotel. Or I'd go to school. By age eleven I'd attended about fourteen *different,* parochial schools—varying Christian denominations, mostly run by the British. There was so much travel at that point, it remains a blur.

First, my mother and I traipsed about France and Italy together, with a brief stay in London. She disliked remaining in one place too long, and was ecstatic to be going elsewhere—wherever she wasn't. Funds were flowing, so she had big plans for our journey.

As she told me, "*Vouz devez voir Paris et lac de Côme.*"[44] She'd spent time in Europe when single, and loved it. We'd visit North Africa, too; my maternal grandmother, now widowed, wanted to meet me. So, Cairo, Egypt followed Paris. My mother's sister, Alys and her

---

43. Julian of Norwich, *Revelations of Divine Love,* Penguin Books, New York. 1966 ed.,
44. "You must see Paris and Lake Como…"

British husband lived in Cape Town, South Africa and my mom wanted to visit. None of this thrilled me. I was (am) a homebody who likes staying put.

Lake Como was spectacular, or so it seemed from the hotel window. All I remember was reading. My mom shopped or met with old friends. For me, being alone was a luxury.

In Paris, my mother and I sat in sidewalk cafés, watching people. She introduced me to my first *café au lait* and the flakiest, most scrumptious buttery croissants imaginable. We had little to discuss. Was that when we both realized we didn't share many interests? The food, the trip, and my mother's friends dominated our chats. There were long silences—not the good kind.

I missed my father's quiet, thoughtful manner, his wit, and the way he'd tailor his big ideas to my understanding. When, for instance, I fell out with a friend he'd say, "If you have two or three real friends in a lifetime, consider yourself lucky. Don't worry about fair-weather types who'll vanish after a disagreement, or reject you in tough times."

Once, I asked him whether God exists. He said, "That's too important an issue, and *I'm* too important to you right now to answer. My words must seem like law to you. It's *your* job, and it looks like it'll be your pleasure, to think deeply about all your religious questions." I loved his honesty, and realized why my dad's friends called him a "straight-shooter."

When I had my own advisory firm, I wished he could have heard the CEO of one Fortune 500 company tell a colleague: "She's a straight-shooter, closed-mouthed, trustworthy."

My mother's mind was exceptionally keen, and never linear. She gave fresh meaning to "thinking outside the box." Her rather primitive, instantaneous read of others was at once penetrating and purely visceral. One take and she knew if a person, a line of poetry, or music was superb or vulgar. She may have been the most complex, original person I've ever met. Refinement of every sort was her métier; yet instinctive comprehension of things made her seem at times quite earthy, quite animalistic.

Art, design—the aesthetic realm—delighted my mother. Even at her worst, when unable to groom herself properly, her posture, manners, the placement of a vase or spoon, revealed that, in spite of internal tortures, she actualized *beauty* in her every move. That grace was who she really was.

She did not, however, share my ardor for the beauty of *ideas*. We could discuss paintings, the latest fashion, cuisine, but not books or philosophical concepts such as were in my readings.

Little Women and *The Diary of Anne Frank* were rich with values about family, injustice, freedom of the kind I craved—not freedom as license, but independence to express in concrete terms the vision and vitality one discovers for a whole life of superordinate meaning. That was my excitement—then and now. It fell on deaf ears.

Our days in Europe were the first time my mom and I had been alone for an extended period. Her energies flowed from a different order of engagements than mine. Thus, although my mom wanted me to go everywhere with her, mostly I begged off. That pattern, begun in Shanghai, grew, persisted, despite an undying love between us.

BACK TO THE MIDDLE AGES

My maternal grandmother made a great fuss. She kept stroking my face and hair (which I detested). Mémère, while affectionate, had been respectful of my "space," so this was way too familiar, way too soon—oppressive, as though I was an object, not an individual in my own right.

My mother seemed ill at ease as well. Her mother (whose name I forget, and may not have ever known) was ancient-looking, somehow forbidding. She appeared as if in mourning—wearing a long, black dress; her hair (black) was sprayed stiff; a shiny helmet pulled straight back, coiled up high from her gray face, a figure from a bygone era—like Midieval times. It's hard to imagine my graceful mother surviving in that dark, spooky house.

The furniture was painted coal black. Touring dimly-lit, airless rooms, one found no life at all—no cats or dogs, not even a goldfish; no plants, no books, not even a radio; no music, no light. My mom and I spent most of our time sight-seeing around Cairo which, by contrast, was modern.

The pyramids came first. I rode on a camel, much preferring horses. The saddle was a deep seat, wood I think, with a large "horn" or handle as in Western saddles, but huge. The camel knelt for one's mounting. When it stood up, it swayed side to side, and the ride itself was bumpy. The camel's face—its lovely eyes and plump horsey lips—made it seem sweet, but I'd never want to ride one again. A year or two later, when invited to ride an elephant, I instantly declined. Enough is enough.

The Egyptian people were charming, gracious, exceedingly polite and friendly. Physically, I thought them beautiful—the men included. It's no exaggeration that their jet-black eyes and exquisite courtesy made me rank the Egyptians amongst the world's most cultured, attractive people. However, one measly week in my maternal grandmother's home was plenty.

A MATURING TRIP

On the return to New York, my mom was "unwell." Something about being in her childhood's environment upset her. It was impossible to get a straight answer as to what was wrong. Quite literally, her speech sounded "crooked"—uneven, illogical, with many twists and turns; so fatiguing to try to follow her train of thought.

Again, as in Shanghai (after my dad was interned as a P.O.W.), my mother was distracted, spoke wistfully of the past—vaguely, with no clue as to the problem. Soon, she was caught in the undertow of old hurts, unable to focus on our visas, passports, or travel. She put herself into my hands, while I leaned on the airline's help. Amazingly, the trip worked out.

As we sailed over the clouds, it dawned on me like a premature sunrise: I loved my mother, but, self-protectively, determined to stay away from her. I trusted myself and sought to freely, fruitfully use my mind, the ideas that seemed sacred, gifts received from God, without supervising an unpredictable adult (who was, often, much like a very young, disruptive child). Trying to distance myself, I said not a word about that. As Madam had taught me, some things "...maybe are best kept to oneself." Would a better, more virtuous daughter have warmed to the caregiver's task? (I thought so.)

A deeper, unspoken truth emerged on that flight: I felt uneasy—unsafe—with my mother when she was disturbed. She "acted out," was angry, unruly, seemingly a danger to herself and others, like me. When my gentle mother became hostile, she was a stranger. Self-protectively I stayed away. What child can admit such feelings to a beloved parent?

As her condition worsened and her dependency grew, the rest of the family withdrew. Which enhanced my guilt. The role-reversal was untenable. I didn't know how to care for her. Worse, I didn't want to supervise anyone. I loved to make things happen, to create things, share gorgeous ideas with those who'd use them. Even then, I wanted to benefit others by thinking, saying, or drawing something fresh, *fruitful,* out of my prayer-life, my imagination, out of existence itself.[45] Soon came the premonition that the situation wouldn't last. An inaudible voice within urged, "Be patient, for now."[46]

HOME AGAIN

Mercifully, my dad met us at the airport and my mom calmed down. Did his presence soothe her (as it did me)? Or, did she want to please him, to show him her ability to function? Either way, she came back to earth.

We remained in New York all spring and summer. Anthony was home with us on weekends. We leased a three-story brownstone near what I was told was Mayor La Guardia's home, called Gracie Mansion. Our house was a dignified red-brick affair, solid and permanent looking. I liked it a lot, except for the steep, dismal stairs that led to the bedrooms. Anthony delighted in sneaking up behind me as I went upstairs. He'd pretend to be a vampire, lightly touching my shoulder, eerily singing my name. I'd scream.

---

45. William Blake believed imagination was not a state but the essence of human existence itself.

46. Studies indicate that many, if not a majority, of children with a mentally ill parent are left in the dark about their parent's condition, feel guilty , and/ or traumatized by the experience. A few as psychologist Maya Piness' research shows transform their lives, becoming highly adaptable, resilient, "invincible" as a result of the experience.

He'd laugh. It was a ghostly staircase, perfect for older brother-younger sister teasing.

For a short time that spring, I went to a new Catholic school. It was good to be in a structured setting. We wore pretty navy blue uniforms—kind of starchy—with crisp white blouses. Like Madeline (in the book of the same name), I walked with other girls to school and felt grown up. This was third grade.

In various countries, I'd had many nuns as teachers. The ones in New York were among the best: serious; brainy; business-like. One could study in silence—my favorite atmosphere. I admired the Sisters and wondered what it might be like to join a convent. Repeatedly, I dismissed that thought as it surfaced. The prayerful attitude, study of Scripture, and orderliness of vowed religious life had enormous appeal. But, no, there was something hiding in mind, something not yet revealed—entering a nunnery was not part of the program.

Around this time, I'd read a book about unmarried women in the Middle Ages who lived alone in a worshipful, scholarly fashion.[47] They functioned in positive, community-supporting ways: Praying for others, strengthening the spiritual life of their church family. Assuming that sort of role was a stirring idea; it seemed right for me, and a service to God. All this came to imagination—appearing now and then, as if in a mist of fantasies. I could see myself living alone, a cat or two winding around my ankles, praying in that wordless transcendent way I'd adopted.

Lately, I'd begun to bury my head in a book, instead of converse with my mom, who then called me "selfish." We were obviously not on the same wavelength about

---

47. These women were called "anchorites," or, in one particular era, "Beguines."

what had value. By asking to read without interruption, I *knew* I'd invite criticism. I also knew what I loved to do, and couldn't see why such a sensible activity was wrong. A friend later explained: "When you don't do what others want, they call *you* selfish."

Concentrating—as when reading or riding horses for hours—was energizing. Using my capacities to the full brought me to life. For example, certain subjects in school— history, literature, language—were endlessly absorbing. Conversely, when someone told me I should like a book or class, I balked. Since early childhood, particular with religious matters, bull-headedness took hold. Around my seventh year, one incident at a favorite school taught me that, in certain cases, my usual timidity lifts, and I answer solely to God or conscience; the law of Life being etched within.[48]

A MEANINGFUL WALK

The "selfishness" issue between my mom and me vanished as soon as a problem cropped up at my new school. This time, my mom was my champion. A short time after I began third grade she got summoned to the principal's office. Although I really enjoyed that school, I noticed that the prayers we recited weren't precisely rooted in Scripture. Somehow it felt wrong for me to *feign* the worshipful stance.[49] Added to that was the indignity of being forced by anyone to pray. (And in public yet.) I was praying all the time, although I lacked words to describe that. Anyway, the recitation was intrusive and, for me, a false witness.

---

48. Isaiah 30:21; Romans 2:15
49. Romans 14:23 comes close to this idea, although St. Paul is talking about eating foods we think are wrong. "If you do anything you think is not right, you are sinning." (New Living Translation)

By refusing to "pray" the verse, apparently I was disrespecting the rules. In fact, while at seven I couldn't explain myself, obedience to the sacred unction of the Holy Spirit forbade me to go along to get along. The verse was not born "of the Spirit."[50] I'd have just stood in class quietly, but that silence wasn't allowed.

The headmistress gave me a choice: Either accept a spanking in assembly (or some such communal arena, for extra humiliation), and then say the prayer. *Or*, go home. I nearly laughed. What a no brainer.

My mom rushed over when called. Hearing the issue, she immediately withdrew me from that school, scolding the principal: "You don't deserve to have a child like Marsha in in your care."

I couldn't believe my ears.

As we walked home that morning—and I'll never forget how bright, clear, and bitingly cold it was—my mother, tears in her eyes, was clutching my hand. She spoke very seriously, very coherently. She totally understood, apologized for enrolling me there in the first place, and talked as to an adult. I got the feeling that she'd been abused or frightened by power-loving, authority figures in her youth. Her empathy seemed rooted in direct experience. That episode illustrates the best, most enlightened side of my mother, the sensitive, devoted, maternal side that stands out in my mind when considering the individual she really was.

Throughout her life, particularly when she was well, my mother intuitively understood that idea of writer Albert Camus, "Nothing is more despicable than respect based

---

50. John 3: 6-8 ("The flesh gives birth to flesh, but the Spirit gives birth to the spirit...")

on fear." She and I had many disagreements, from which long separations ensued. Nevertheless I shall always treasure my mother's example and influence in this critical respect: It was she who reinforced my innate sense that I have a right to be who and what I am, and to feel what I feel. No small gift. No minor lesson.

Did my dad ever hear about that incident? I wasn't told. It wasn't the first time I'd been expelled for similar reasons. Since he was wary of organized religions, he may not have minded. He never said a word about it.

Before long, my parents and I left on another trip. Again, Anthony was ensconced in military school. So came long years of family separations.

BOMBAY[51]

At first glance, India looked rich. Beneath its vibrant surface, it was poor. Throngs of people bustled about, many women wearing pink, saffron and brightly striped saris; animals—dogs, cats, chickens, even cows—roamed the streets freely amidst pushcarts laden with jewelry, food, and trinkets. Cars, cabs, bicycles jammed thoroughfares. It seemed a city packed with too much of everything. But the poverty, such as I'd never seen, was stunning. Waifs of every age—mostly barefoot—crowded around tourists, begging for alms or anything handy. Some seemed like preschoolers in threadbare clothes; some babies were naked.

My dad had been in India for a few months; his business there was thriving, and he had many new associates.

---

51. Bombay was renamed Mumbai in1995.

Having leased a suite at the classic "Taj"[52] hotel, my parents told me we'd be living there for about seven months to a year.

When we stayed put for two or three months, I'd usually be sent to a British-run school. For some reason, in Bombay, I had an outstanding Indian tutor which may explain why he was retained. He was droll, had a polished Oxford accent, and loved books, ideas, learning. We got on famously.

Most of my tutors, including this one, used a program called the Calvert System—a good thing, since no matter the tutor, with Calvert the lessons were consistent.[53] Bombay's back streets and passageways offered another course of study. I was now old enough to wander about alone.

MY NOVEL CLASSROOMS

Long stretches arose when I wasn't studying. The travel itself was an advanced course in human relations, cultural nuances, body language, and finding my footing amidst strangers. Today, I'm a homebody who prefers her creature comforts. At seven and eight, I was an adventurer, learning to trust my own intelligence, which, early on, I saw had less to do with "book smarts" and much more to do with *street* smarts. Certain capacities we develop by being thrown into unknowns. Such as those in foreign lands.

The latter skills I'd liken to the improvisational powers of surfers and skateboarders. They keep their balance

---

52. The hotel may now be called "The Taj Mahal Palace." I have not seen it since childhood, but remember our stay fondly. That is where I first stayed alone in the suite when my parents went out in the evening.
53. Calvert Schools or educational system began in the early 1900s. See: www.calverteducation.org

while continually repositioning themselves on moving platforms. Their focus, stability, flexibility reflect a high, steady consciousness. Maneuvering the back passages of foreign cities built similar, if more subjective, adaptability. It turned out I enjoyed testing myself in those fluid situations. As with the thrill of riding horses, one never knows exactly what will come up.

Solo excursions into the wilds of new locales gave me much needed confidence. The older I got, the more sure I felt when investigating an alien territory. I'd leave the hotel in the morning with nervous anticipation, and return after lunch bolstered by the conversations I'd had with shopkeepers and all manner of strangers. How better to gain interactive skills? It was so much fun to try out my few known words of an unfamiliar tongue, more fun still to join in with the glee of those who helped me pronounce phrases that I'd mangled. And then there was the food.

My mother warned me not to eat anything from street vendors. Seduced, I ate my fill. How could anyone resist the sights and scents of sugary cakes, ice creams, or spicy curry in pretty, hand-painted dishes ? In Bombay, vegetarian dishes such as deep-fried potatoes mashed with rice and chutney, piled into flat bread sandwiches were like burgers and hot dogs in New York. I devoured heaps of flat, fluffy noodles in green leafy wraps, rice and vegetables. Everything was tantalizingly displayed on bamboo and silver trays. I bought tasty assortments from all the street carts, and never got sick—just chubbier with each passing month.

In one sense, I was shielded by privilege, protected by nannies, tutors and boarding schools. In another, I was exposed to novelty of persons, places, experience. Fortunately, when traveling, I could explore by myself, the mysteries of the back streets. *That* was school.

There were fearsome situations. I'd get lost. I'd need help. Strangers showed me the way back to the hotel. Street urchins, some quite tough-looking, much older than I was, crowded around begging for coins, sometimes confrontationally. A few were scary, laughing, poking, pointing, often touching my blond hair and fair skin. Things always turned out well if one stayed calm, looked people straight in the eye as friends, and had faith in the reciprocity of simple goodness. It's doubtful I'd have fared so well if I hadn't felt a real fondness for those lovely boys who initially seemed so threatening. I believe we're all keenly perceptive; you can't fake liking the other guy who can't fake noticing what you really feel. Of course these were simpler, less angry times in simpler, less angry places.

Then, too, I stayed alone in hotel rooms for hours. My ever anxious mother hovered annoyingly before she and my dad left for an outing. Her insecurities increased mine. Conversely, my dad built courage with his instructions, "If you need anything, call the front desk. You always know what to do. So trust your judgment; it's very sound." What powerful words. I never needed to phone the front desk. No surprise that it felt second nature when, later, for years, I traveled alone for my own firm.

After Bombay, my parents needed to scout business locations. My father was still heading up his own import-export company. All I knew was that geo-political conditions influenced what he could and couldn't accomplish. I flew to California, to the first of a few boarding schools in the L.A. area. Supposedly, I'd be near my aunt and uncle. My hope was to visit infrequently.

SCHOOL RULES ~ STOMACH RULES

The all-girls school (around Pasadena, I think) was agreeable. There were no bullies. Having to share sleeping quarters, closets, and bathroom with others was hugely unappealing, but a trifle. What haunts me to this day was a profound homesickness. I missed my family intensely—feelings I can summon up at will to this day. Given the proximity of others, the noise and lack of privacy, my prayer-life morphed into a silent "pondering" of one or two lines of Scripture. Sometimes I prayed while walking, and also in the shower. Thankfully, I was not expelled. There was only one close call.

The unfortunate incident involved meal-time. The law was that all of us tiny guests were to eat up everything served. Our tall, lanky headmistress had a long, beak-like nose, and salmon-colored hair (too bright and brassy to be natural). She roamed around the lunch tables making sure we'd consumed all our food, a task she took very seriously.

One day, in her rose-colored smock, looking like a towering flamingo, our keeper abruptly stopped by my seat. Pointing a thin finger at a heap of stewed tomatoes, she ordered, "Please eat all your vegetables, Marsha." With heart pounding, I politely explained that tomatoes in any form didn't agree with me. Her pinkness insisted, "You *must* finish."

With the expulsion from various schools in mind, I obeyed. My throat locked, innards churned. I swallowed a forkful of soggy red mush. Whereupon, amidst my gleeful, wide-eyed classmates, reflexively I threw up all over our good steward. Glaring at me, she spun around and breezed out of the dining hall.

The other girls assured me I wouldn't get thrown out. After all, *I* didn't rebel; my innards did. They were right; I stayed on.

LESSONS AND INFLUENCES

My mother's response to her own mother taught me a lot about women of old. They seemed hostages to their parents' demands, required to fulfill the role they'd been assigned. I shuddered at the thought of that captivity.

Travel, boarding schools—these cemented my love of relaxed small-talk with people I didn't know. Strangers felt much like family. From seven to eleven I grew in self-direction, but ,within, was far from peace. Despite ongoing prayer, insecurity battled with the resolve that my inward listening increased. I'd heard that small still voice since my beginnings. Yet, once in America, feeling like an oddity with relatives, noticing tensions between my father and brother, observing my mother's impairment, and *always* craving a freedom that seemed blocked by her dependence—all that demanded wise guidance. And not from my elders (my dad excepted). Even getting lost in new cities, finding my way back to hotels by sensing which strangers to trust, shaped my current life.

There is nothing unusual here. Most children *learn* to respect their own judgment when push comes to shove. That seems the wholesome norm, the wisdom or discernment that saves us when it counts. It's essential for contemplatives, or anyone else who thrives on independence, to have discernment. That's a life-skill. My *inward listening* habit developed whatever such skills I had.

BREAKING NEWS

While at boarding school, Aunt Jeanne and Uncle Jack's house was my weekend residence. Over time, I preferred to stay at school; however, the occasional weekend with them was unavoidable. Despite their welcoming efforts, I felt like an intruder. After all, it's not easy having a child disrupt one's routines. Besides, a weekend at school, in my room—especially with the others gone—was a treat. Some children feel lonely when by themselves; I didn't.

At my relatives, I met Uncle Jack's cousins, but could never figure out if (or how) we were connected. They seemed overly clannish, a quality I find closed, darkly unappealing. What a Godsend when Uncle Albert was around. There was a bond of affection and light-heartedness between us; we'd been family since my infancy.

Jeanne and Jack's two sons completed the usual crowd. We gathered at the pool, and I swam nearly all day. Jeanne arranged a lavish buffet outdoors, served up copious portions of stuffed grape leaves, pilaf studded with pine nuts, hummus, and pita sandwiches. The swimming parties, delicious food, and sun-drenched days did not offset what was to me like an inordinate tribalism. As outgoing as I was with strangers in foreign lands, that's how alienated I felt with this group. Like many children, I wondered "Was I adopted?"

One balmy weekend, my aunt and a companion were chatting in the room in which I was reading. Patting the chair next to hers, Jeanne said, "Come join us." Her unremarkable friend, making small talk, asked, "So are you and your half-brother keeping in touch while you're in school?"

Half-brother? I froze. The hair on the back of my neck stood up.

Jeanne gave her friend The Look that said, "She doesn't know yet." Too late. The truth was out. With heart in throat, I sputtered, "What do you mean?" Much hemming and hawing ensued as Jeanne spilled the beans: "You see, your father was married once before. His first wife died soon after Anthony was born. Then your dad met your mother, married, and they had you. So Anthony is your half-brother."

The *half-brother* term stunned me. Fleeing the room, I demanded a return to school. My poor aunt didn't know what else to do.

Anthony and me in New York

Jeanne must have told my mother immediately because, in a week or less, our headmistress informed me (with no displeasure) that I was to join my parents in Thailand. On that flight I decided Anthony was my true brother, no matter what others said. After which, I felt fine. The tiniest turn of mind can make such a difference.

❧

Chapter 5

CHILDHOOD'S END

"…the transcendent state is the crown of our ascent toward Reality." —Evelyn Undderhill [54]

Alovely blond stewardess kept her eye on me. For a time she sat in the empty seat next to mine to ask, "You've flown alone before, haven't you?" Nodding, I answered, "Yes. I'm joining my parents in Bangkok." She smiled and added, "Your father wrote to the airline, most precise about how you were to be supervised. Few parents take such care." Her remarks made me happy.

My father's actions were loving, yet he internalized his feelings. He traveled across the world to see me in boarding school, and did the same for Anthony. He was prompt, never missed a scheduled visit, and somehow always managed to ask about my interests. My classmates warmed to him immediately. I was so proud of my father.

"THE LAND OF SMILES"

On the way to the hotel in Thailand,[55] my dad listened while my mother softly explained about Anthony: "You were too young to discuss such things with. We're sorry

---

54. Evelyn Underhill, *Mysticism* (New York: E.P. Dutton, 1961 edition), 34. (Paraphrased)
55. Thailand or The Kingdom of Thailand was formerly called Siam.

you learned about Anthony as you did." I nodded glumly, struggling not to cry, and understood.

What bothered me most was imagining how Anthony must have felt. How severe might his loneliness have been? He'd been shuttled off to schools for so long, his education being paramount to my dad.

Years later, when we finally saw each other again, Anthony and I spoke of all this. We agreed: We were truly brother and sister—none of the rest mattered. Yet how amazing to realize that my big brother, who enjoyed tormenting me, had never revealed a word about our having different mothers, despite knowing of it since he was a very little boy. No small feat.

Our Thai hotel was surrounded by a mix of modern office buildings, hotels, and rickety, wood-framed shops— little stores and stalls squeezed into every inch of every nook. The business district was a warren of hallways and doors cut into interconnected walls of yet more shops. The thicket of food stands vied with each other for space. Talk about enterprise.

Our suite was huge, with ever-spinning, ever-useless ceiling fans. Thailand is hot and humid—muggy even at night. The "wet season" brings rain in sheets. Consequently, Bangkok is lush, green, rich with bright lilies, wild orchids, gigantic mangos and papayas juicier and sweeter than anything we in the West taste. *Klongs* or waterways, provide transportation options as well as more opportunities for yet more little foods and flowers. The *klongs,* studded with mostly handcrafted teak, bamboo, and wood-planked fishing vessels presented a charming, if jam-packed, shopping scene.

The Thai people were helpful, welcoming, physically lovely—save for the elderly, many if not most, of whom had badly stained teeth from chewing betel nut.[56] Their joviality and sweetness made one forget appearances. Beauty shone through.

Below and in back of our hotel was a ménagerie, or little wildlife atrium. It housed small monkeys, green parrots, bright red and blue macaws; these colorful birds, as well as snakes and lizards are all plentiful in Thailand.

MY TENDERHEARTED FATHER

On entering the flat, I was surprised and delighted to find in my dad's den, a jet-black mynah bird with a bright yellow crest behind its eyes.[57] It was hopping from perch to perch in a spacious aviary. By its side, in another gigantic cage, a slow Loris[58] peered out with brown, globe-like eyes. Both cages had tree branches for the animals' comfort. My father had arranged to "foster" the creatures for the downstairs ménagerie.

Without exception, our entire family adored animals. Until Thailand, however, I had no idea how strong my dad's rapport was with them.

Once, after midnight, I arose from bed to investigate voices. There, on the floor of his den, sat my dad, teaching the mynah bird to talk. The two seemed in perfect accord. I've since learned that mynahs readily speak to

---

56. Chewing the nut was, during my stay, a practice in Southeast Asia dating back to the 1st Century A.D. Many countries have the tradition of eating areca nut mixed with betel nut (or betel leaf). The nut is actually a berry, and despite the lengthy custom (and symbolic sense that this mixture fuels love and happy marriage) in recent decades the ritual chewing has declined.
57. The mynah is probably not a good pet. It is now one of the most invasive birds in the world, and threatens the ecosystem and even human interests wherever it lives, mostly Asia, India, and Australia.
58. The slow Loris is a small, nocturnal primate.

(and imitate) people who give them the most care, feeding, and attention. Soon that bird sang out, "Cheerrio"—my father's very Briitsh "goodbye."

Once more at night, hearing sounds, I got up to find my usually dignified father, reclining on the carpet beside the Slow Loris' cage. The little primate was hanging upside down on a branch, its round, owl-like eyes fixed on my dad's face, who in turn was cooing to the Loris in that high-pitched voice one uses with infants. Noticing me in the doorway, my dad shrugged sheepishly as if to say, "I can't help myself—it's so cute."

My father painted beautifully. Repeatedly, after we'd all gone to bed, he'd sit at an easel, working with watercolors to capture an image of a full moon shining on the street below. He and Anthony were so alike in artistic skills. Father, however, kept his painting under wraps, expressing his creativity in entrepreneurial outlets. Such observations convinced me that countless gifted entrepreneurs are really *business artists.*[59]

Eventually, my parents leased a home near a famous gold-roofed temple. We returned the zoo creatures to the menagerie. Another troupe of animals appeared at the new house.

THE ART DECO'S GECKOS

Our leased house was a two storied, art-deco style with bright white walls and high ceilings, and a small den for my dad—the only air-conditioned room. Whenever possible, the three of us spent evenings there. My dad

---

59. Early in my career, I developed that idea, e.g., "Entrepreneurs, Chaos, and Creativity—can the highly creative survive large company structure?", *Sloan Management Review,* MIT, Winter, 1985, Vol. 2.

worked at his desk; my mom would knit; her needles clicked away expertly while she gazed elsewhere. I'd lie on my stomach, on the floor, reading. We were cramped in that little room, but it felt safe, snug, and rich with pleasure.

We had three Siamese cats—moving sculptures they were, charmingly smart with distinctive yowls; the place came with two oversized Airedales—wiry, friendly guard dogs, not pets. There was a black lab for me, named Monkow. Which may mean *crown.* Monkow was the sweetest-tempered dog I'd ever known. You could set a tea-cup on his pancake-flat forehead without spilling a drop of tea. We were inseparable. (When we left for the States, I missed him as much as any human friend I'd lost.)

At night, along stark white walls, freely roamed tokay lizards (geckos). One here, one there, all frightful looking big lizards, helpfully hunting (and devouring) the plentiful atrocious insects of humid, tropical Thailand. At first, I found all that unsettling. I decided that it was far better to see tokays slithering on walls nightly than to find horrific bugs scuttling around our floors at any time. Luckily, snakes remained outdoors.

MY INSCRUTABLE MOTHER

In Bangkok, my mother displayed a purposeful side I'd not noticed often. The event that elicited these traits occurred at my new parochial establishment. Possibly run by Seventh Day Adventists, it may have been called the International School.[60]) The students were Americans, British, and other Europeans. All of them and the teachers

---

60. I believe there are other schools with this name.

were friendly and polite. That was one of my favorite school experiences. A relaxed, democratic atmosphere prevailed. Happily, I wasn't thrown out.

A pedicab[61] took me to and from school daily. I'd then take the same one to go horseback riding. For security reasons, my dad had retained one driver, a wiry, wizened man, to transport me everywhere. From the back seat, I'd fixate on his corded grapefruit-sized calves, made huge from constant cycling. Bangkok, in my experience, was safe, despite occasional conflicts between the military and elected government. Those tensions erupted from time to time, when hostilities were high. As far as I knew, none of these disputes involved the Europeans or Americans.

One morning, before recess, we students found our parents crowded in the hall near the front office, waiting for us. Mother looking serious but composed, told me, "Your father is away, so let's go quickly. There's been a *coup d'etat* in the city and it's dangerous for you to ride home alone."[62]

As we rode in the familiar pedicab that was waiting, she cautioned me, "When we pass soldiers, look straight ahead. Make no sudden moves and, if the soldiers stop us, just smile and be quiet. Do not, under any circumstance, argue with them or try to protect me." I nodded, imagining she was thinking about my having tried to fight the armed military men in Shanghai.

The driver peddled confidently through deserted streets where only pockets of uniformed soldiers stood

---

61. A pedicab is a tricycle with a two or three seat bucket "basket" in the back.
62. The coup in question may have been the "Silent Coup" in November 1951, which would have been about six months before we moved back to the U.S.

holding guns. As the guards turned to stare at the raven-haired Caucasian and little blond girl moving by in the open-air cab, my mother smiled sweetly. She raised her hand in a regal wave—as if the Queen Mother out for a ride. One soldier seemed primed to wave back, caught himself sharply, and gave us a sober nod. We sped by without incident.

With her wits about her, my mother—to borrow poet Rumi's phrase—possessed the unfathomable grace that charms birds out of trees. This happened at the start of a lengthy rough patch for her, yet she'd had the presence of mind to handle things masterfully. Her clarity and protectiveness made her subsequent incapacity all the more poignant. I wonder what might we each become without our various soul-sicknesses.

THE FEARLESS MRS. KOCH

I had a daily riding class. The school was owned and operated by a sturdy, ruddy-complected German: Mrs. Koch. Her exacting standards and eagle-eye caught every practice that might harm either us or the horses. We rode usually in a ring, saddled and unsaddled our horses, rubbed them down after our rides, and sometimes cleaned out their stalls. Mrs. Koch never delegating supervision to older students.

Here was an independent, *single* mother—the first I'd met. She owned a business, supported herself and her daughter who was about my age, capable and tough. We became friends of a sort, although I can't recall her name. We only shared one interest: horses. She rode splendidly.

In those days, single motherhood was uncommon. With the exception of my mother's friend, Zazi, in New

York, and Madame in Shanghai, all the women I'd known were married (or had been), and were mothers. Mostly, husbands or sons supported them. Mrs. Koch was a novelty. Competent in so many areas, she proved that a woman might carve out a fulfilling life by following her heart's purposes—not society's programming.

I marveled at her practical ability to live as she saw fit. Or, at minimum, to live as well as possible given the hand she'd either chosen or been dealt. At the time, adults rarely discussed their "journey" with children. So how she happened to be in Thailand, running a riding school, raising a daughter alone remained her private affair.

Notions of who was worth studying for future reference crystalized early. By the time Mrs. Koch entered the scene, I knew her character had value for further scrutiny. Apparently, there was more—or at least something vastly different—to women's lives than was being expressed by the ones closest to me.

I began keeping a mental scrapbook of possible paths for my future—picking and choosing roles and qualities because of some preexisting seed or *inborn* image firmly planted within. Certain lives hinted of that idea. For instance, since I always sought more courage, virtue, more "strong faith" (like Abraham's), Mrs. Koch demonstrated those traits in feasible, everyday terms. Here was a superb riding teacher *and* a model of self-rule. I regret that I never revealed my admiration.

The riding itself was rematkable. A small group of us rode daily through paddy fields (rice cultivation areas, largely on wetlands). We'd race each other, darting along narrow paths that wound above swamp-like grasses where herds of water buffalo grazed. Those docile, magnificent creatures made for exhilarating rides. Seeing those huge, placid animals was a thrill. Despite their easy-going nature, their size and treacherous-looking curved horns could scare anyone. The harmless beasts glanced up, unconcerned as we galloped by, then resumed their foraging.[63]

We rode on English saddles, and were expected to sit straight, use our knees, voices, and reins to guide our mounts (not the whip). A seasoned rider lets the horse's gait in trotting, running, or jumping have its natural show of athleticism. Being small, I preferred riding a pony (about fourteen hands[64]). For competition riding, my horse was over fifteen hands. Riding, for me, was meditative—a seamless, telepathic rapport between rider and horse that seems greatly under-acknowledged. Yet that affinity is a critical feature of the sport. When, for instance, my horse and I were in sync during high jumps, it was transcendent. Of two types of people—those who easily enter such states, and those who can't—I belonged to the former.

Our riding school held practice competitions to prepare us for larger gymkhanas.[65] Before the first regional show, someone asked Mrs. Koch to leave me out because I wasn't competitive enough. She refused, saying, "Marsha may not have the 'killer instinct', but she's very focused, has a special bond with horses, and strives to outdo her previous record. She stays in." That was the only compliment I'd

---

63. I think the water buffalo is herbivorous, grazes on the aquatic vegetation in the paddy fields, which restores the integrity of the wetlands. More people depend on water buffalo than any other domesticated animal. They are truly glorious.

64. A pony measures 14.2 hands (53 inches at the withers); a horse is over 13.2 hands.

65. The Anglo-Indian term for a contest of sports games, usually conducted by sporting-clubs, to display the skills and training of participants in equestrian maneuvers, such as dressage and jumping.

ever heard from someone outside my family. What a confidence booster.

My parents attended the competition—the first (and last) time either saw me perform in anything. Although I was uneasy about their being there, and shaky about riding in front of a crowd, the jumps required the fullest engagement with one's horse. Once my turn came, all nervousness disappeared. my horse and I performed within what seemed a protected bubble. As we jumped, I heard no sounds, no shouts, no applause, just total transformative stillness, absolute coherence. I'd entered that state only in certain prayers, right before sleep. From then on I sought more of the *silence* of ultimate Reality—the supreme Being or "All and in all".[66] I was nine. I knew nothing about such ideas. I never spoke of this—not until adulthood. Yet, any child can have a *spiritual* sense or soul-longing about these things that linger, like a haunting refrain.[67]

Astonishingly, I won first place in my category of high-hurdle horsemanship. A local dignitary presented the gold cup in front of the cheering crowd. After the ceremony, my father patted my shoulder and said gruffly, "Well done. Good show." My mother cried. She later said, "Your father is very proud of you." I knew that if he'd told me himself, he'd have choked up with emotion. (And I'd have wept.) In our family, body language exposed feelings.

ENVISIONING A FUTURE

On special occasions, when she had time, Mrs. Koch and her daughter invited me to dinner. We gathered around

---

66. Colossians 3:10-11

67. Saintly children, according to *Saints and Society* (op cit) do, in fact, *express* such ideas and aspirations in unequivocal terms that often shock their elders.

their kitchen table at their little home. Here was the warmth of a permanence which I craved. And glorious scents drifted from Mrs. Koch's specialty: Spaetzle (a German dumpling) and chicken soup. Where had she found time to cook?

Not until my thirties did I have the courage to pursue the spiritually set-apart life I'd felt called to live. Mrs. Koch helped me imagine some traits needed for that. Both she and her daughter were tough. I was not. Of course my mother's delicate manner shaped my bias about femininity. Yet a fuller, more complete integration of "soft" and bold qualities was essential, like the strong faith that is less timid and conforming than I was. I wanted to work in a robust, "giving" way. In my creaturely state, I felt ill-equipped for that.

Once I asked my dad how he knew who, in business, to trust. He answered, "Trust your instincts when it comes to agreements. You'll make mistakes, but don't worry, that's how we learn. Trust the handshake, the character of the person—not the promises of those who talk too much or too fast." I couldn't wait to try out such instructions. I knew I trusted him and Mrs. Koch.

Around the end of 1950 and for the duration of our stay in Thailand, rumors were in the air that a war was brewing in Vietnam. (Thailand and Vietnam are about an hour and a half apart by plane). The Communists were encroaching. Our household help, and shopkeepers that I'd come to know, worried that the conflict would spill over into a pro-America Thailand.

I'm assuming that the gathering of war-clouds concerned those with U.S. business interests—like my dad.
Given his POW experience, he was eyeing the door marked
"Exit" to a safer life. Was his more immediate concern my
mom? Melancholy was her new norm.

Her old symptoms returned: distractedness, emotional
distance, and new to the mix, apathy. Many days she simply stayed in bed. Could she have been clinically depressed?
She lamented, incoherently, about some vague trauma long
passed. I'd taken refuge in school, horseback riding, or
sometimes at Mrs. Koch's house, so all this was hardest on
my dad.

My father first sent my mother and me back to L.A.
(where Anthony was now in military school). A distressing
time ensued.

PRE-PUBESCENT TRIALS

When we came to Thailand I was nearly nine; now,
almost eleven, I longed to be with my friends, to live in one
place. Thailand had been a welcomed respite from constant travel. I loved the people, my school, Mrs. Koch; I
adored my dog, Monkow, my Siamese cats, our home. The
possibility of venturing further into competitive riding was
tantalizing. The past two years had revealed a depth of
understanding about my parents that I hadn't had before.
I was learning about myself as well. Bangkok was home.

Nevertheless, back we went. I was unhappy being
alone with my mom, but learned long ago to keep such
concerns to myself. We found an apartment, and I stayed
in my room as much as possible. Any mother as sensitive
and perceptive as mine senses what her daughter feels.

There was palpable tension between us. To worsen matters, money was tight.

No one told me—my parents never spoke of finances. It must have been a worry. The hotel in which we first stayed, and the small ground floor apartment after that, felt grim. My mother had an "episode" at the interim flat. An ambulance was there when I got home from playing and, for a short time, I stayed with my Aunt Jeanne. Eventually, we moved to a pretty, albeit small, duplex in what we heard was the "not-so-good" section of Beverly Hills. I was enrolled in one of the four local elementary schools, and ultimately that was my escape. But not at first.

"WELCOME TO PUBLIC SCHOOL."

Compared to my other schools—small, bungalow structures in rural settings—the brownish-brick building looked ominous, rather like a penitentiary. It was a dark, forbidding, three-story affair with mostly hard surfaces: shiny hardwood floors and stairs; concrete playground with all steel slides, climbing bars, metal swing sets with blackish-leather seats. The cement handball courts sat at the back of the asphalted property. One or two spindly trees, barely alive, stood in squares of dry soil bordered by yet more concrete. It was the harshest setting I'd ever seen.

The staff gave me a placement test, clucked sadly over something they called "deficiencies in math and science," nodded approvingly over my aptitude for language, analytical and abstract reasoning, and put me in sixth grade. Having just turned eleven, sixth grade seemed about right.

The principal took me up wooden stairs, walked me through a long, windowless hall smelling of cafeteria cooking—pea soup or boiled ham—opened a brown, wood door with a little square window at the top, and led me into a classroom of eyes.

"Boys and girls," he announced, "This is Marsha. She's come all the way from Asia, and she's never been in an American classroom before. So let's welcome her to public school." Thirty some children, mouths gaping wide, sensing fresh prey, stifled laughter. I turned beet-red, wanting to run. A twig-thin, white-haired teacher—Mrs. Dunker, I *think*—came over, took my cold, sweaty hand in her warm, papery-dry one, and showed me to a seat. On the verge of tears, "Please, God," I prayed, "Don't let me cry."

The long and short of the next, two-year stint was this: At first, I was teased and ridiculed for speaking with a British accent. It didn't take long to rid myself of any trace of that. I was bullied by some cloddish girls. At the end of each day, I'd go home crying to my mom, only to hear that "things will get better." She had her own troubles, so mine must have seemed trivial. (Not to me.) As was my way, I prayed at night, cried at night, slept fitfully, and dreaded leaving for school each morning.

When something had gone wrong in Shanghai, Mémère philosophically converted the Biblical saying, "It came to pass," by reinterpreting it: "This has come in order to pass." The bullying did pass.

Within the first two months of massive adjustments, I'd cultivated a defensive shield of sarcastic humor. It held the toughs at bay. They weren't sure if I was being snide, or playful. The brighter students enjoyed the ploy. Somehow the gambit let me maneuver between groups.

Mockery (and *self*-mockery) became second nature. When the mean girls—some of whom reputedly had "round heels"—said, "You're weird," about my off-the-cuff remarks, they pronounced it "wired." I laughed, teasing, "Don't you mean 'weird'? The brainy kids snickered *at* the flustered girls. Things improved.

By mid-sixth grade, I'd made friends with the honor-students and the so-called "bad" kids. Truth was, I loved them all, they sensed it, so I freely moved between factions. My boyfriend" at the time (Bill), was like a brother: Platonic. For the rest of my life I never joined a clique or "clan." The little tribalisms of grade and high school, of college, and even the workplace seemed so limiting. Each disparate circle lifted thought to fresh levels. Today, it appears that my non-denominational faith and crossover writer's voice began in early childhood, way back in Southeast Asia's alleyways, while making peace with youngsters who looked menacing, but, down deep, were just like me.

WITH A LITTLE HELP FROM MY FRIENDS

My best friend, Ethel, lived across the street from us. Ethel was a petite, demure, all-knowing girl; my tutor in pre-teen wisdoms, including the birds and bees. (My genteel mother could never utter the word "sex.") Ethel cautioned me about teachers. One seventh grade terror was said to drink alcohol in class, and then threw books at students if they irritated her.

Ethel and a girl named Susan were the friends I trusted enough to invite home. Meeting my mom, they instantly sized up the situation.

Susan and I spent time at her place. Her mom was always home, a pretty picture in a rose terrycloth robe, tiny feet in pink slippers with little white feathers at the toes. Her mother cooked hamburgers non-stop. We three sat around the kitchen table, munching burgers, sipping Cokes, sharing stories. Ethel and Susan (and Susan's mother) took me under their wings.

Ethel and Susan were the first of many close friends I've had over the course of my life whom I've loved like sisters. My "boyfriends" at the time were like brothers: platonic. Bill and I looked alike, what with our fair, translucent skin, light hair—his was nearly white—and an inability to stop blushing bright red when called on in class. Bill, enchanted by the stars and moon and outer space, phoned me at night. We spoke long and seriously about the stars, the meaning of infinity (and eternity), and our futures. Bill was the only one with whom I could discuss my religious views. He may have been an Irish Catholic, but we never mentioned denominations. We were just two youngsters eager to voice long-held, budding notions about God, Reality, the spiritual side of life, and so-called death. His was the first of several rare friendships of that sort that have continued throughout my life.

Again, at the end of sixth grade, I narrowly missed being suspended. Again, the problem related to my refusal to go along with some rule. This time my sin was influencing others to follow suit.

What happened was this: Some teacher—or committee—sent our parents a letter stating that children shouldn't watch tv after 9 PM. It was too late; a few shows were unsuitable for young minds. We older students (sixth through eighth grade) were up in arms.

Most of us watched *I Love Lucy* which aired around 9. My response to our collective fury was to draft a petition saying it was none of the school's business what we watched, or when. By this time, I'd gained popularity with all manner of students; almost everyone in grades six through eight signed the pronouncement, with my name big, on the first line.

When I was summoned to the front office, the principal said, "Marsha, you seem to have started all this, so you concern me most. You need to put your leadership to better use." He then sat me down on a wooden bench outside his office and phoned my home. This time, my dad answered and was invited in for an official chat.

My dad's footsteps echoed as he marched down the hard floor of the long hallway. Without so much as a glance at me, he strode into the principal's office, spent a moment, appeared again—furious—and raised his chin toward the exit, silently ordering, "Let's go."

During our drive his icy quiet was my greatest reprimand. I said, "I'm sorry, Daddy." No reply. When he finally spoke, he said, "Never sign a petition unless you understand the long-lasting consequences. One's name stays on a petition for God knows how long. It's serious, serious business."

It dawned on me that the religious intolerance and political tyranny he'd known in childhood—certainly that of his prisoner-of-war years in China—had made him ultra-cautious about opposing government authority. My having instigated a formal complaint against a state institution must have unnerved him. My father was more fearful for me than angry *at* me.

I was so sorry about having caused him a moment's grief. It also must be said that I no longer hold such views. (When, decades later, I became a principal, I offered the same no-late-TV advice to parents.)

The rest of sixth grade, the summer, and most all of seventh grade was uneventful. Susan, Ethel, Bill, and I found ourselves placed in the same class with a Mr. Shaeffer, thankful that we'd missed the homeroom of the teacher who threw books. Bill and I continued our esoteric phone talks at night, including discussions about various mystical notions. Ethel and I, still best friends, were now enthralled with the same "older" eighth grade boys. Their names changed weekly. Susan and I strengthened our after-school ritual of heading for her home each weekday. Her mother was ever present, ever cooking hamburgers for the three of us. It had become our ceremonial, after-school snack at a white Formica kitchen table that heard a lot of girlish gossip for about a year.

By now, Anthony had graduated. He was home, and we were all still at the two-story duplex. He'd changed. He was handsome, worldly, seemingly unconcerned about his future. This, I could not understand.

Apart from genuine affection, he and I shared only a related humor—not much else. We'd spent the bulk of our young years apart, each of us shaped by different forces. We clashed in ideas, goals, temperaments. Unlike Anthony, my future held untold fascination for me.

LESSONS AND INFLUENCES

John Donne's poem, "No Man Is an Island," reminds one how knit together we are in diverse, eternal ways. The longer and more wholesomely we live in solitude, the clearer becomes our love and need for each other. At least, for me, school and riding classes (in Thailand), and close friends in California enriched adulthood immeasurably. How differently would things have been without these early "best friends"? How lonely, had I not by disposition, thoroughly *enjoyed* all variety of others? High school, college, teaching, and business gratifications were made possible largely because of the pure fun of being with people. Contemplatives tend to be social, not isolates. Indeed, emotional well-being in contemplative life, whatever its form, depends on a past that is rich and healthy in friendships—and a present rich and healthy in love. In youth, I kept a whole lot to myself; not until mid-adulthood did I learn to open up about my interior world.

More: my one riding competition, where I scaled high hurdles in the Transcendent zone, affected me profoundly. From then on, even with the distractions (and hormones) of my teens and young adulthood, the *substance of silence*[68] was alive within. Who could be contemplative without that? I've insisted that only God makes contemplatives, yet deep prayer and meditation open the door. [69]

AND YET MORE CHANGE

I can't say when my mother first went to a sanatorium, but before long—sixth grade had not quite ended—Anthony and I were alone in the apartment. We got along well, and as mentioned, I spent most waking hours at school and at friends'.

Mémère was still living with her other son, my Uncle Roger, therefore my dad was on his own. Now he had to reinvent his ideas of parenthood, and certainly his livelihood. Either because of my mom's condition, or the political tensions in Asia, or both, my dad needed a new type of job. He'd never worked *for* anyone before. He retrained

68. Max Picard's phrase.
69. Revelation 3:20

himself as a stockbroker thus altering his life. Instead of running his own firm—being free to travel at will—my creative father became an independent agent, probably on commission, in a small L.A. office. Whenever possible, he worked at home in our living room. He was no hale-and-hearty salesman. For an intellectual, an inventive, thoughtful man, the new position took its toll.

At night, my father paced the floor or played solitaire until dawn. He drank and smoked excessively, worried and heartsick about my mother. That scenario went on for over a year. Despite gaining a modicum of broker success and a new group of pals with whom he played poker, this wasn't what he'd had in mind for himself.

He began pressuring Anthony to get a job, expecting his only son to contribute to the household expenses. Before long, Anthony took a part-time position selling dresses at a posh Rodeo boutique. My brother's wit, elegant—perhaps glib—manner, and unsurpassed taste charmed everyone; soon he had many wealthy acquaintances. None of that thrilled my dad.

As seventh grade ended, so did my mother's stability. My parents separated. My mom first went to Aunt Jeanne's, who must have felt overwhelmed. In truth, I expected myself to shield those I loved from pain. In fact, I felt helpless, then guilty for not knowing what to do.

Right before my thirteenth birthday, at the end of seventh grade, Ethel and I walking home from school, saw an ambulance parked in front of my apartment. Emergency technicians were rolling someone out to their vehicle. Heart racing, I ran to the stretcher, expecting to see my mom, even though she was away. It was my father, pale, skin glistening with perspiration. He saw me, mumbled something like, "Don't worry, Marsha, it'll be alright."

Two days later, my father, age forty-eight, died of a massive heart attack. With that, our exotic little family expired as well. Thus endeth childhood.

My Father

&

PART III

LIFE SET APART

Chapter 6

SCHOOL GIRL ~ SHOP GIRL

*...nothing was certain, and promises were made only to be
broken. School life provided a dimension of security, a stable
routine, and a happy freedom from the domestic dramas...*
—**Alec Guinness**[70]

The funeral was held at a chapel, the burial at Forest
Lawn. A minister no one knew said something I didn't
hear. Total strangers—various business friends of my
dad's—patted my back and spoke solemnly. They seemed
to reverence my father. A few remembered how much he
helped them after the War: One said, "Your father was the
most moral man I knew." A heavily-accented man told me,
"Your papa brought some jewelry of ours back to the States.
We only shook hands on this. He could have kept everything, but put it in a bank box until we could lawfully claim
it." I didn't understand. It was clear though, and no surprise, that my dad had helped a lot of people, honorably.

Until then, I'd not met my father's California friends.
Given my mom's condition, none of us invited anyone to
visit. If my mom asked, "Why don't you invite your school-
mates over?", we'd protect her feelings with some pitiful
excuse. She knew why.

At the funeral, an attractive, teary-eyed woman introduced herself as "Esther." Her husband, Paul, glumly stood

---

70. Alec Guinness, *Blessings in Disguise* (New York: Warner Books, 1995), 27.

by. She said, "Your father played poker with my husband. He was a great friend of ours. We'll miss him terribly."

Esther was warm and friendly. Before leaving, she promised to phone me when things had sorted themselves out. Anthony and I returned to the apartment, distraught. Like someone who's been in an accident, yet recalls nothing, we felt uncharacteristically little.

The day I walked back into my class, Mr. Shaeffer joined me in private to say, "We're all so sorry to hear about your father. If I can do anything to help, please don't hesitate to ask." I nodded, starting to cry; his sweetness undid me. He was the only adult at school who'd had the courage—or interest—to say anything caring. My three darling friends, Ethel, Susan, and Bill stood near me. Bill had no words; Ethel, that intuitive little mother, stroked my arm, but said nothing. Susan nudged me back to her house after school where her mother waited, cooked cheeseburgers, and we three sat in the kitchen at their Formica nook , eating quietly. Experience said these were friends that, again, I'd have to leave.

Anthony and I remained by ourselves for a week or so. Where my mother was, we didn't know. Frankly, her absence was a relief. It sounds harsh but she needed looking after. Neither of us could manage that. Anyone who has lived with a mentally ill loved one may empathize with such contradictions. For us, love warred against self-preservation. The mentally ill, for all the care and support they require, can be quintessentially self-absorbed. My mom's ranbling—what psychiatrist Thomas Szasz once called "a chopped salad of words"[71] drained our energy.

---

71. Thomas Szasz, *The Second Sin* (New York: Anchor Books, 1984), (possibly paraphrased).

Anthony and I sat in that duplex, wondering aloud what to do. Both of us were too shell-shocked to weep. We realized our days together were over. In a week or so he joined the military—I don't recall which branch.

I was listening inwardly. From my depths sprung the injunction: "Leave now." Where could I go? I prayed hard, with emotions I didn't understand.

THE DROPPING OF THE OTHER SHOE

Days later, my Aunt Jeanne's oldest son arrived for a talk. There was good news: My father had left a sizeable insurance policy. He'd apparently intended the money as a cushion for the family if something happened to him. There was enough for anything we'd need, including a modest home and an education for Anthony and me. I had already decided that I would not live with my mother under any circumstance, but did not want to live with my relatives either. My cousin sensed that, or maybe I spilled those beans. Or (probably) my aunt and uncle had coached their son about discouraging my living with them. My aunt must have been reeling with dread at the prospect of a preteenager moving into their home. Who could blame her? She'd just finished raising two sons. My cousin and I agreed: Boarding school was the ideal answer.

Before I could take a breath, my cousin shifted uneasily in his chair. He cleared his throat. To the wave of relief that had washed over me, Intuition whispered, "Not so fast, kiddo– there's more news coming."

He continued, "Your mother insisted on taking the entire sum in order to travel around Europe." I froze. "Does she expect me to come along?"

More throat clearing, more body shifts. Ah, silly me: She'd already left. (I didn't recall her saying goodbye.)

The upshot of my cousin's visit was positive: He'd managed to set aside enough money for me to attend a college-prep boarding school. He'd take me there in a couple of days. Since Anthony didn't want to go to college, there'd be enough for my tuition through high school. After that, I'd be on my own.

Politeness forbade my mentioning that my mother's departure was a bonus. I'd sown the seeds of an intentional vow, about going it alone—a response to that soundless "voice" within that had said, "Leave now." Mémère's caution, way back when, reverberated in mind: "Don't look back. Obey that silent heart-nudge that says, 'Go to the left and to the right.'" Selfish or not, guilt-ridden or not, I decided I'd never live with my mother again. And never did. (There's something to be said about sticking to one's guns.)

Was it strange that I didn't blame my mother for leaving ? In fact, I blamed myself for preferring to be on my own. Today, I imagine my natural flight from a fearsome situation was the *same* self-protective instinct as that of my mother's.

In fairness, who'd fault her for fleeing? I understood her plight, exactly as I knew she understood mine. The wordless mother-daughter bond is mysterious. I'd have run, too. What with psychiatrists and those closest to her nipping at her heels, planning to imprison her, to perform God only knows what atrocities on her to get her well. In escaping, she was crazy like a fox, evading those who'd take her very life. Remember, these were the days of lobotomies and shock treatments. I was rooting for us both.

Being one who cries easily—at sappy ads, corny movies, and most any farewell—I didn't cry much; not at the news of my father's death; not at his funeral; not afterwards. My relatives made the financial arrangements for my next few years. I remained peculiarly mature and sensible about everything.

Except: At thirteen, I didn't know enough about money to inquire about the insurance sums. How much precisely did my dad leave? How much was in my school account? Who was managing the money and how? I never asked. To this day, I've never sought an accounting. The money aspects were the least of my worries. Whatever obstacles my financial privations put in my way seemed irrelevant. Weirdly enough, in awhile I was glad for the strengthening of will, autonomy, determination, and practical know-how that grew out of that time.

I felt I was carrying precious cargo in the form of God-given capacities: a sense of destiny, talents, intelligence, a real love and deep understanding of people. A true *joie de vivre*, and much more, God had provided. It would have been a sin to squander such wealth. I had to leave.[72] Early life had been secure; adolescence less so; my teens, scary. Passive, I was not. I'd wanted a way out, and got it. Blessings in disguise.

THE SILENT TREATMENT

Between the day my cousin told me about my mother's departure with the insurance money, and the day he

---

72. Gen. 2:24; Eph. 5: 31: I believe there are times in life, when—joined to God, or "hearing" from God—we are obligated to move into the unknown, leaving family and the world we know for that summons. I suspect most of us are called in this existential way. Few obey.

dropped me off at the boarding school, a lone event stands out. One night in my bedroom I began to pray, calmly admitting my anger. The longer I spoke, the more fury grew. Why had my father—a good, sweet, virtuous man—died? Why had my mother gotten ill? Anger, it is said, is rooted in fear, but I didn't *feel* fearful then. Just enraged that someone as loving as my father was no longer with us, that my gentle, graceful mother was so disturbed, now so at risk of being mistreated.

That prayer lasted moments. It ended with my telling God that, since prayers were useless, I would stop. ("Why have I been praying for my parents and Anthony all these years? What's the point?")

A friend once said he'd become a Christian out of fear of God. Not so for me. Childhood's vivid intimacies and encounters with the Lord, and—yes—angelic, or divine, protective guidance, had given me a surety of Oneness, though not its fullness. (That spiritual sense persisted, however much I tried to ignore it.) From that prayer onward, throughout my teens, I turned away from any outer worship. Still, some blessed thing lived on within.

Decades later, viewing actor Robert Duval in the film *Tender Mercies* as he storms at God, I remembered my tirade. Never afraid of God, I've always believed that forthrightness, genuine honesty is part of prayer *if* we, like Jesus, realize "I and the Father are one."[73] In the worst of times, by faith through Grace— that closeness is never something I've "earned" by virtue. Intimacy with God has been experiential, a radical encounter.

---

73. John 10:30

After my rant, like the Lost Son in Luke 15, I left for a distant land. Until my early thirties, I was very much *of* the world, not merely in it.

However, I did not say there is no God; did not feel alone; never stopped experiencing God's presence. In a frightened, childish huff, I simply gave God the cold shoulder. More: I concluded that from then on, I'd keep private things private: No one needed to know about my spiritual sensibilities, insights about relatives or their place in my life.

Natural spontaneity and a desire to connect with others made such restraint hard to pull off. I *still* work on the art of self-control. There's wisdom in that old Italian saying, "Never reveal the bottom of your purse or the depth of your mind." That rule worked well, for a while.

HACIENDA DAYS

The new school was not a worry; I'd survived umpteen different placements and a swarm of tutors. How bad could a small, private setup be?

In fact, it was a dream. My tirade at God forgotten, I now thanked Him for a match made in Heaven.

My cousin and I drove up a long, circular driveway behind which stood a low-slung, red-tile roofed, Spanish-style structure. It was an estate on five or more acres in what was then rural San Fernando Valley—a suburb of L.A. . Edged by tall, fragrant Eucalyptus trees, at the back of the school stood–Glory be!—a stable with one palomino and one brown mare. Two friendly, tan and white boxer dogs, slobbering profusely, padded out to drool over us.

Accompanying the dogs was a tall, sun bronzed man; handsome, graceful, smiling. He introduced himself as "Kent," headmaster and proprietor, then showed us around. The girls' dorm—upstairs—held seven or so beds. With its wrap-around veranda overlooking the back garden, it gave us a view of a riding ring. Behind that were stables. I thought, "This works for me."

Aloud, I asked, "Can students ride? I love horses." Kent smiled, nodded, adding, "My dad, Mr. B., takes care of all that. Let him see how good a rider you are." Gladness surged.

Kent moved like a dancer, which was what he'd been before opening the school. His parents had been vaudevillians as well.

Based on initial tests, Kent placed me in the ninth grade, meaning I'd skipped eighth. I wasn't freakishly young for the placement; my birthday, in late May, meant I was merely one year younger than my peers.

Years later, it dawned on me that this was a 9-12 high school. There was no eighth grade; Kent *had* to put me in the ninth.

A LOVE OF LEARNING

My grandmother was right: Watching over me must have been my guardian angel. I'd been "led" to the ideal school. No legalisms here.

The movie *Auntie Mame* illustrates my high school's *avant-garde* climate. The eclectic, eccentric Mame's motto was, "Life's a banquet, and most poor suckers are starving to death." Our lessons were a feast! We didn't memorize facts, per se. We devoured a sumptuous spread of classical offerings : film, music, literature. If we students didn't love learning before enrolling, we surely did after.

Our classes were tiny, individualized—much as home schooling had been in China, and then with the Calvert system. Many of my classmates were the offspring of actors and producers, some child stars (one a well-known teen singer) and a few, like me, whose parents had either died or were busy elsewhere. No one was impressed with their or anyone else's status. I'd guess each of us was pre-occupied with private concerns. We got along well. Kent's relaxed manner and focus on learning prevailed. And none of us in that small, friendly group—many boys and girls who lived under the same roof—ever confused others for family. We were just pals.

In sunny weather, some teachers held classes outdoors. We sat on the lawn with our books, discussing our readings, trying to get the teacher off the subject. We regularly attended USC's movie series—cinematic classics, such as *Gaslight, All Quiet on the Western Front, Diabolique*. We watched Charlie Chaplain and Buster Keaton films, and more. Undergirding our studies, those outings—and all manner of field trips to museums and art exhibitions— were the constant blitz of one idea: College was essential for each of us. It wasn't simply to make connections, find a good job, or a spouse. No, knowledge developed the whole person. This wasn't school—it was a celebration of learning.

Two summer field trips to Mexico were part of the program. Kent leased a home in Cuernavaca, and we made side-trips to Acapulco, Taxco, Mexico City, and Vera Cruz. Only ten or so students went. Because I boarded full time (i.e., all holidays, summers, weekends) I'd have to go. Only occasionally did I visit my aunt and uncle, but the trip required signed approval of a legal guardian. That's when

I discovered, I had none. Aunt Jeanne refused to sign the permission slip, which involved guardianship.

Someone looked the other way, because I went.

We drove down in two cars—Kent's beige Cadillac and his father's station wagon. By the end of the summer, I'd fallen in puppy love with one of the older boys ("Sheldon"). We held hands in the car. Quite thrilling, really.

Near the end of that first year, Aunt Jeanne sat down with me to talk. ("Oh no," I thought, "Now what?") Her news was that my mother was back, had exhausted the insurance funds, and was at my Uncle Albert's tiny flat. "There's no more money for your school." Worse: "She's unwell," my aunt continued, "and will have to go back to a hospital." That was my mother's greatest horror. My heart sank. We were all powerless to do anything, as are all families of the mentally ill—a much neglected, long-suffering lot.

According to Aunt Jeanne, my mom was scared, angry, unpredictable, and a danger to herself and others. I'd witnessed these signs before. She smoked in bed when depressed, cooked meals while in manic states, and in other ways put any household at risk. Albert, the most even-tempered one among us, refused to be around her. Each in our own way felt heartsick.

Considering my options, where and *how* would I live? I was afraid. Here was the sort of crossroad where one can lose one's way. "I'll get a job, but must stay at school," I informed my aunt, wondering who'd hire a fourteen year old to do anything. She shrugged as if saying, "Maybe." I knew Kent would help.

Kent was a "healthy" or clean communicator: no mixed messages, no sly double-entendres, no creepy manipulations. That plain-spoken educator also avoided ultra-authoritarian lectures. I trusted him.

"Don't worry about tuition," he said. "For now, there are funds set aside. You help Dad, maybe with the stables and horses, maybe something else—he's aging, and it will be good for him. If money falls short, we'll call it a partial scholarship. You're going to college and that's final." He agreed: I could also work part time somewhere, after school.

The notion of having a job was wildly appealing. The sheer purposefulness of work—being of use—seemed built-in and right for me.

Once again, I did not think to ask about how much money was left in my school account, or how much originally had been set aside. I trusted everyone. I still don't know the figures.

"WE'LL SEE HOW YOU DO."

Within days, I'd interviewed for a clerk's job at a nearby five-and dime on Ventura Boulevard near the La Reina Theater.[74] My future employer's gaunt face was kindly. Here was a middle-aged, stoop-shouldered man, with a sloping, care-worn stance. I'd watch him in his white, short-sleeved shirt, moving bruskly through the aisles, glancing at shelves with head down—probably to avoid eye-contact with anyone. I imagine he didn't want to hear complaints.

The interview centered on my background. Enthusiasm took hold and I talked too much. The store owner listened,

---

74. A 'five and dime' was a variety store, offering a wide assortment of products, such as cosmetics, art, sewing, and school supplies, and some had lunch counters where one could buy sandwiches or other light meals. A great concept.

stared at me, then gave a nod: "Let's see how you do—you start next week. Every afternoon."

Oh joy! I reported the good news to Kent, who patted my back. "Good. Very good." He was pleased; I was over the moon.

Gold letters on the tomato-red sign, proclaimed: "Five and Dime." The store was about three miles from school—an easy enough walk. Kent, or his father Mr. B, must have taken me to the State Employment Office to get a work permit and social security card because I reported to work immediately.

INTRINSIC PLEASURES

I'd found my niche in stocking shelves, polishing jars, problem solving. Here was tangible success. My people-skills blossomed in the easy banter with customers and co-workers. I enjoyed sales, and basked in the freedom of that job. I had huge chunks of time to think, plan, and day-dream. Daily walks to and from work became the blue-sky seeding sessions that grew my future. And then, there were those paychecks.

A DNA FOR SOLITUDE

I was no ascetic, but those afternoon walks resulted in a sense of oneness with the world. Is that proclivity in one's genes? I felt no "isolation," just tranquility. I strode in the Silence that organizes and soothes the soul. Eventually, I understood the life rule of one early desert father:

"Be solitary, be silent, and be at peace." [75]

The meditative drumbeat of my steps morphed the teenaged angst (or "small self") into another, better, *stronger* self—more real, substantial than who I was when torn apart by external, hindering voices. To coin Maslow's phrase—solitude brought me a sense of "just-rightness."

These treks left the imagination free to picture possibilities. Being inherently talkative, solitude also curbed my often inane chatter, thus preserving energy.

Much like hearing a Bach concerto, dancing, or even washing floors—a mindful walk helped me dissect problems into manageable bits.

Whether or not I'd stopped talking to God didn't seem to matter. God hadn't stopped talking to me, especially as I trudged along and also before I fell asleep at night. I was listening. Somehow my responses to people—friends my age, customers at work, my teachers—seemed motivated from within. The more I heard interiorly, the better things went. (I regret to report, I frequently ignored that prompt.)

Another bonus: My walks exposed an inward listening *practice;* an intimate communion with the presence at my very ground of being. At fourteen, I felt this was unique to me—unaware of a *universal pattern* in those called to contemplative life: Often a reflective person's routines are invaded by sudden clarity that shows God's Is-ness is the *only* Real, the undergirding dimension of existence.[76] That sense inserted itself into my daily doings.[77] Such instances began to dominate my worldview, and must account for

---

75. Ward, op cit. That was the *rule of life* of Abba Arsinius.

76. Deut. 6:4

77. For a variegated look at the pattern, see Thomas Merton's *The New Man* (New York: Farrar, Straus & Giroux, 1961), a book that continues to bless me.

the confidence (admittedly shaky) with which I met circumstances. These young years were marked by a wobbly fortitude.

Only gradually did I feel able to solve problems in my own fashion—ignore cookie-cutter advice, trust my own slower, pray-for-guidance method explained by Psalm 36:9, "...in Thy Light shall we see light." In high school and college, that Light was often dim due to my distractedness.

For example, not until my thirties, while on retreat at the Visitation Monastery in Washington State, did I begin to integrate my love of solitude with a love of being with people. Even so, that merger wasn't automatic.

The skills and strength to form, then arrange, my current contemplative life (however relaxed), flowed more easily after spiritual direction, lengthy rounds of worshipful routines. The retreat (and there were several) revealed the kind of days I wanted. Yet, I was not meant for a monastic life.

An invaluable spiritual director once explained the "mixed life" to me: You are fully devoted to God, yet fruitfully engaged with life. You are simply "not of this world"—social or solitary, you give from your gifts. "

IT'S EASY HAVING GREEN

Each week, I was paid by the five-and-dime. Each week, I immediately deposited those checks. Banks then gave savings customers little brown, leatherette account books. For each deposit, tellers wrote in the amount, added the interest so total always grew. How satisfying. Best of all, the account was *mine*, no one could take it, and unlike the ambiguous sums of insurance money, I knew to the penny what I had.

That first year at the dime store, I was put in charge of the cosmetic counter. By high school's end, I was managing several counters. Each promotion brought a few cents raise —which, when saved methodically, accumulated to a hefty bundle for college. I now felt I had options.

Of course, there wasn't a whole lot of choice when one made a dollar or two an hour, but having money of my own let me *feel* as though I had, *or would have,* alternatives. I could already taste the feeling: "I'll do this and not that, because I prefer it, and because I *can*." The hubris of youth.

In fact, I was ultra-sensitive, acutely aware of the financial thin-ice on which I stood. Nevertheless, single-minded resolve built that little savings, thereby enabling me to attend, and complete, college. Today, I thank God that, to quote St. Paul, "I would not be disqualified for the prize."[78]

"AND A HIGHWAY SHALL BE THERE..."[79]

Around the end of high school, Anthony wrote to say he was being discharged from the service because of an unspecified problem. A month later, he moved into a house in Hollywood with two friends. He found a job—waiting tables—and seemed happier. Within weeks, he'd bought a car and invited me over for the weekend. Kent gave permission.

On the way, Anthony explained that he was gay (at the time, a mystery term to me). He described what that

---

78. 1Cor.9:24-27
79. Isaiah 35:8

meant, and said it was why he was discharged.[80] Pretending to understand, I genuinely didn't care so long as my brother was alright. Unfortunately, that weekend was traumatic for me: He and the others drank too much. The first night's noise and intoxication were chaotic, upsetting. Another speedy return to boarding school. Anthony understood, but thereafter there was a gulf between us. I suspect he knew it was the excesses, not particularly lifestyle issues, that bothered me. Even a young child knows what's right for *her.*

I chose consciously to travel on that invisible highway that Isaiah describes.[81] To be frank, in my thirties I myself took corrupting detours. Yet, progressively, as will be clear, sought out a narrower path.

LESSONS AND CONTEMPLATIVE INFLUENCES

No matter how much I preferred my own company, after my dad's death it felt good, healing, *necessary* to let others be supportive. School provided structure, consistency, a level-headedness that I sorely craved. Friends helped me deal with financial worries in the way only teenagers' humor can. From about thirteen to sixteen (when I graduated from high school) my head spun from so many defining experiences, as two examples illustrate:

First, nothing prepared me for my father's death. Ethel, Susan, and her mom were in my corner. No family member comforted either Anthony or me. Thus began premature adulthood. It wasn't difficult because I *felt* so little. I'm not sure about Anthony. He must have been in shock, scared, insecure. The two of us just sat around numbly.

---

80. Before 1993, there was a ban on homosexuality in the military.
81. Isiah 35:8

Second, my aunt's refusal to sign guardianship papers showed me that I wasn't the center of the world and not to ask too much of others. There followed the self-reliance for which I'm grateful, considering the alternatives. My headmaster Kent's good shepherding balanced the scales: He was one of many who showed up when most needed and least expected, the one of two "grown ups" who stood in for my dad for a little while.

Since casual contemplatives live spiritually amongst the secularly-minded, they'll need an intuitive sense of how best to get along—even when it seems impossible. Faith works wonders. Contemplatives don't strive for *self*-perfection; they're learning how to live The Great Commandment-whether in a family, a school or a cloistered community.[82]

LET'S SKIP THE CEREMONY

In tenth grade, Kent administered the Stanford Binet I.Q. test to our whole student body. With testing done, he took me aside, told me my score, adding, "You're ready for college now. How would you feel about skipping the eleventh grade?" I felt delighted. By sixteen, I'd applied to U. C. L. A. , and felt ready to graduate. I soon wondered if Kent accelerated me because of financial constraints. No matter. U.C.L.A. accepted me. (Hurrah!)

That summer, Kent drove me to Westwood to assess college housing and take more exams. Accommodations turned out to be a sorority, less expensive when compared to the dorms, and in most respects familiar, being much like boarding school.

---

82. Matthew 22: 35-40, :The Great Commandment is actually two in one –to love God with all our heart, mind and soul and to love our neighbor as ourselves.

The sorority was a palatial, two-story home atop Hilgard Avenue. One could cut through what were U.C.L.A.'s park-like Botanical Gardens, walk a short way, and be in class.

Rush week seemed silly, a fawning bid for approval and membership. Ever practical, I eyed the benefits, and tried to impress. Sorority life offered safe, clean, up-scale lodgings. My "sisters" would be bright, polite, refined. A very good deal if one could pass the superficial muster. I could.

In truth, our members were wonderfully smart, caring, good-humored.

U.C.L.A. had about thirty-thousand students; my high school's senior class was about twenty graduates. The size didn't faze me; it felt exciting to be part of that vibrant, lovely campus—an expanded state of mind, an eye-opening, intellectually stimulating frontier. Here was a new world calling us youngsters to explore uncharted territories of thought, and perhaps even discover ourselves. I couldn't wait to start.

Days before high school ended, my mother was released from the hospital. She moved back with my aunt and uncle, and made loving, needy overtures for a warm reunion. I'd heard that tune before: "No one understands but you. Stop this college business. You get a job, I'll take care of you." As if.

When my mom promised to attend my high school graduation, I arranged to skip the whole affair. We got together only after I was well ensconced at U.C.L.A.

Our reunion was tense, tearful, emotional. And short. Soon after, Mother left again. How she financed these trips, I had no clue. I just knew that my paltry savings were enough for two semesters, and that I'd earn more.

I'd saved every cent of my wages. The few adults sur-rounding me—Kent, Esther and Paul (the couple I'd met at my dad's funeral), perhaps my aunt—gave me graduation gifts (i.e., money). I banked it all, having already started work at U.C.L.A.'s Main Library.

There wasn't a sweeter bunch than my supervisory staff and co-workers at the Catalogue Department —my workplace for four undergraduate years. The job? Filing subject heading cards.

"*Never look back,*" my grandmother had said. Kent's rule was identical. On our last drive to Westwood, we hardly spoke, knowing it was unlikely our paths would cross again. He had new students to guide. I had new adventures to tackle. Letting go is the first step; That's most of my battle.

On the driveway of the sorority, we mumbled our goodbyes: some clumsy thanks from me, some encourage-ment and send-off pats on my back from Kent. That was it. Off he went, leaving me, teary-eyed and anxious. So began college.

૭

Chapter 7

TESTED

My hero...is the archetype of the double-agent in all of us. We live much of our lives beneath the surface—like icebergs. Most of our thoughts and desires are unexpressed.

—John le Carré'[83]

Three of us—Barbara, Carol, and I—were assigned to a sunny corner room overlooking Hilgard Avenue. While unpacking, we found common ground in humor and worldview, becoming fast friends. They'd had sisters. I'd had boarding schools, so we were all used to sharing quarters, confidences, bathrooms.

The tall, willowy Barbara, the petite redhead Carol, and I grew so close that, down the line, we wore the same wedding dress. Barbara bought it, wore it first; then Carol, then me. We were blasphemous about the commercial spectacle of weddings. By sharing one dress we (or at least I) saved funds and had fun. Did I ever have an in-depth discussion about God with either, or anyone, in college? It's doubtful. I prayed in bed, nightly.

When the sun hit the windows of our all pink room, the space took on a promising, rosy glow. Which well depicts our mood when we three were together. All of us

---

83. Mattthew Bruccoli, Judith Baughman, eds., *Conversations with John le Carré* (Jackson, MS: Univerity Press of Mississippi, 2004), 86.

were sensitive, funny, impatient with artificiality. It was a super friendship. (Carol and I are still in touch.)

Carol, a Theater Arts major, had a magnificent voice. She sang and acted in many of U.C.L.A.'s productions. Barbara's comic, even-tempered intelligence made her an ideal teacher candidate. I hadn't declared my area of emphasis. There seemed no course of study for one with metaphysical inclinations.

Any irreverent opinion I'd held about sorority girls being vain and shallow evaporated. The vast majority were gifted, refined, and cared about people. On the flip side, it was a fairly conventional lot. I'd guess most of the girls intended to marry, have children, and be full time wives and mothers. (It was the fifties.) I planned to marry, but felt parenting was not in my future. After all, I was already raising a child. (Me.)

My wish was to have a creative, artistic life—something non-traditional had my name on it. Even so, I knew a degree was essential. In that, I was simply edging toward a vision that, as yet, lacked specifics. The hurdles were constant, and jumping these took all my focus.

Looking back, I question how I overcame academic barriers. High jumps on horseback were mellow compared to *these* intimidating obstacles. I agonized over my deficits, mostly helplessness at not being able to help my mother. And I worried constantly about finances.

A KID NEEDS WHEELS

To reach the best part-time job interviews in nearby towns, the buses were useless. With no driver's license, no vehicle, no money for the latter, what could a girl do? One great idea saved the day. Summoning up nerve, I withdrew

126

a little money from my bank account, phoned a local driving school, which gladly picked me up for two or three lessons. Before long, I visited the Department of Motor Vehicles, passed both the paper and driver's test, and shopped for a car. Who, if anyone, signed my learner's permit? Maybe the driving school. It's hazy. Two hundred dollars later, I owned a used, 1950-ish, yellow Buick sedan with a black top.

I'd gone to the lot alone. The salesman could have sold me a lemon. He didn't. That Buick ran reliably for *years*. It lacked power steering, handled like a tank, but never broke down (Amazing Grace.)

Having pre-arranged insurance, even with the Auto Club for roadside help (just in case), all was set. Nervously, I drove off, making a *slow* bee-line for campus. I parked that old car in front of the sorority, parallel to a brand-new, baby blue 1955, first-generation Thunderbird. Some girl's father had given her the iconic car for her birthday. One day, I thought, I'll buy my own Thunderbird. (By the time I could afford it, I'd lost interest.) Turns out, I loved to drive and fast. I had speeding tickets, no accidents, with only one close call.

The near-miss came months later, after visiting my mother. She'd "found" a wealthy, mature (at least thirty) Middle Eastern man for me to marry; she then would live with us, following old-world tradition. Furious that she'd try to "sell me" for her comfort, I drove off in tears, badly navigated a sharp curve on Sunset Boulevard. The car spun into the opposite lane, then stalled. Thank God for no oncoming traffic. Shaken, but unharmed, I was cautious ever after. Though my mother and I always made amends, from then on I kept my distance.

Within the first week of owning a car, I drove into Beverly Hills, interviewed for, and landed, a weekend job at a weekly newspaper (writing obituaries and the weather). Feeling rich, my next stop was Saks Fifth Avenue on Wilshire where I was at home. A lipstick was my congratulatory gift to myself.

The entire operation—learning to drive, getting a license, buying the Buick, finding that second job—took about six weeks. Jobs and money—these were easy. Academics were tougher. Everything was so new.

TOO MANY "FIRSTS"

Lack of funds, a grueling schedule of work and study kept me stressed. The Library took twenty hours per week, babysitting and my newspaper job took weekends. I carried eighteen units of course work, and tried to go to as many parties as possible. There were boyfriends galore. Even with the audacity and energy of youth, I nearly flunked out first term.

Today I understand why I fainted so often, lost concentration during tests, and failed courses: *diet pills,* scrounged from friends.

The plan? To stay awake all night, studying. Sadly, I blanked out during exams. The mix of uppers, sleep deprivation, not eating proved futile. (They're called "*diet pills*" for good reason.)

The classes I enjoyed most were Dr. Hans Meyerhoff's philosophy, and one called Western Civ. In Psychology, we studied Abraham Maslow's exhilarating ideas. Conceptualizing being a breeze for me, subjects such as literature, history and philosophy saved my academic skin. I failed

"Dumbell English," passing it in summer school. No sparkling scholar by any means.

Not until graduate school, years later, had I the luxury of getting an education without having to work. Only then did I become engrossed in study—"better late than never" applies.

Running for classes with thousands of others was a first. Taking notes, sitting in giant halls alongside hundreds was a first. Studying under professors who didn't know, or care to know, one's name was a first; nearly flunking out of school—all these were firsts—a tad too many for comfort.

Then, too, I was the first female in my family to (a) attend college or (b) work outside the home. My plate of firsts was piled a bit high.

I'd set my sights on finishing college. Something *good* inside, something higher, wanted release. It was more vast and significant to me than conventional life—but what was it? Mystifying as that "something more" was, I pressured myself to keep going. Sometimes, you just forge ahead without knowing why. Kierkegaard wrote that when we cling to the Good against all odds, this unifies us with all others. Feeling that unity, an indescribable inner strength seemed to say, "*This*, I will do."

Hard work, and intense thought-work—these were right. I was most myself when, say, examining abstract or metaphysical ideas. Envisioning a creative, contributive life, (however foggy its form), I'd felt something within affirming, "This is truly me." I never heard "voices," just a wordless utterance.[84] Early on, a *closer-than-breath* directive surfaced during, perhaps after, prayer or contemplating

---

84. The Bible refers to *'rhema'* as that which is spoken, instructed, God's directing interior utterance, usually but not exclusively a line or verse of scripture.

some issue. In college these spiritual apprehensions reinforced the will to press on.

ONE HABIT, ONE QUESTION

Friends who know my background ask, "How, as a
teen, could you know your right course of action?" I've
noted one practice—probably cultivated before five—of
"listening inwardly." Some inborn temper and my grandmother's encouragement let me acknowledge the subjective realm.

From that habit sprang one guiding question, helpful
chiefly (but not only) in youth. When in doubt, I'd ask
myself, "If I had a beloved child, what would I advise she
do in this circumstance?" A sound reply followed.

One example: In college, a handsome medical student
invited me to a fraternity party. While there, he got drunk,
became overly familiar, even brutish. Alone in the hall, I
wondered what to do. Listening inwardly, from deep down
bubbled up instruction: "Think how you'd want your own
daughter to act now." I phoned a cab, quietly leaving,
without a goodbye.

After my father died, alternative parents surfaced.
Esther, the attractive woman who'd consoled me at the
funeral, was one. Her bright, playful husband, Paul, was
another—a father figure whose life I soon consciously
planned to emulate.

ESTHER AND PAUL

Esther and I often lunched together, developing an
easy rapport with an adult flavor. During high school, I'd
spent many holidays and two summers at their Cheviot
Hills home—an upscale residential district in West L.A.

Their cozy home had a sunny white kitchen, two luxurious bedrooms (one was mine when I visited), and two miniature Schnauzers who seemed quite human.

Paul had retired early —in his forties—from a trucking business. He'd had one goal: To golf every day for the rest of his life. Which he did. Justifiably, their home was nestled between two golf courses—Rancho Park, a public venue, and the exclusive Hillcrest Country Club.

Each weekday morning, Paul put on his "uniform"— old tattered khaki Bermuda shorts and an olive drab t-shirt, and headed over to Rancho Park to meet his golfing cronies. Before leaving, he'd call out, "I'm off to the office." That spirited curmudgeon could have joined the country club, but enjoyed poking a finger in the eye of all who took pride in their status symbols.

Certain family members had lightly regarded my confidences. Never those two. Having been manipulated in all the usual and unusual ways, I'd cultivated a sixth sense about the untrustworthy, and avoided such types. Because I trusted Paul's advice, I took one of my highest-paying (most noxious) jobs.

One summer, while staying with Esther and Paul, a photo lab offered me full-time work. It meant sitting in a windowless (i.e., airless) closet-sized room, splicing negatives in the dark with a razor. I'd dip the film strips into foul-smelling chemicals, thereby breathing harmful fumes for hours. Getting to work was even worse.

The lab was a long, hazardous trek from Cheviot Hills—over two congested boulevards. I nearly refused the job. Those meditative high school walks to work had been along rural roads. Motorists ignored me. Now as a self-conscious young woman, I loathed hearing cat-calls from passing drivers.

When Paul heard the salary (many times more than the Main Library paid) he said, "The walk won't hurt you. Do what you must, within the law, to support yourself. You'll be glad next term when you see your bank account." He was right. I took that and other awful jobs (like selling brooms, door to door), and with satisfaction watched my savings grow.

If things got tough, I'd hear Paul's advice: "If you're tired, rest up. When you can, get up. Then keep going."

BLESSINGS UNDISGUISED

Study took a back seat to earning enough to pay bills. The diploma, not scholarship, would let me support myself and help my mother. Between the library, weekend baby-sitting, and off-campus jobs, there was precious little time for classwork. (I made time for boys.)

Baby-sitting paid little, but it was such a pleasure. Children and I were in-tune. Among my repeat baby-sitting clients was a lovely family: Ed, a math professor, his wife, Vivian—an erudite, literature major—and their infant daughter, Raun. One evening, Vivian asked if I'd like to meet her brother, Ray Sinetar. He'd recently returned from the army, and was in law school at U.C.L.A. I agreed to meet him.

In a week, there at my door stood a handsome, soft-spoken Ray. Over dinner at Trancas, a romantic Malibu restaurant, I learned my date was exceptional: bright, articulate, hard-working, morally elevated. Ray described his family, the part-time job at his parents' West L.A. liquor store and his law school studies. He hoped to be eligible for "The Order of Coif," an honor society for U.S. law school graduates in the top ten percent of their class. (He did make Coif.)

We shared similar values, a solid work ethic, ambitions, sympathy for the underdog, dislike of pretension. Viv and Ed were prescient: Ray and I were well suited. Soon we'd met each other's families. Only my mom was displeased.

She realized if we married, we'd be broke while putting each other through school. I explained that, as we got on our feet, we'd help her financially. Again, her mental health suffered. Her symptoms convinced me that, for some, mental illness is rooted in an inability to deal with life—as if their guiding lights don't work, leaving them in the dark.

OF WEEPING CELEBRANTS

We were married in the company of about fifty family and friends. A rabbi officiated, Anthony walked me down the aisle. Uncle Albert cried; Ray's parents cried; my aunt and uncle cried; Esther cried; I cried. Tears of joy.

My mother looked as if in mourning. When I grasped that she'd gained weight, could fit into just one black dress, I cried some more.

For "something borrowed" I wore my roommates' communal wedding dress.

After a short, splendid honeymoon at Lake Arrowhead, a resort-village near L.A., we took up residence in a tiny rented bungalow close to U.C.L.A. Ray resumed his law studies—riding a bike to campus, working on weekends. My full-time job was as an office-manager for a Brentwood architectural firm.

Honeymoon at Lake Arrowhead

Intense study for the Bar began. Ray toiled alone each night, and on weekends with a few classmates. They crowded into the small second bedroom we'd converted into Ray's den. The young men strategically divided up subject areas—tax, torts, criminal law and such—according to some preset tactic. Endlessly they'd quiz each other on possible exam questions.

All of them passed on the first try.

Most became prominent attorneys. Ray, a legal scholar at heart, advanced quickly in his field of criminal law. He was a fierce litigator whose oratory talent, dogged competitiveness, and unrivaled will to win soon made him a lawyer's lawyer. I was so proud of him, and his parents fairly oozed fulfillment.

Our first years were happily productive, signaling a propitious future. We threw ourselves wholeheartedly into marriage. Ray studied. I worked. We took turns cleaning our apartment—Ray being the neater one. Rising at dawn on Saturdays, we marketed, ate breakfast at cheap diners, entertained. Glad early days.

Ray's mother, Adele, was my confidant. We shared an intuitive sense about people , and felt protective of them, having both been hurt by our mothers.

Al and Adele met and married in New York after arriving separately from Hungary. Adele's stepmother abused her; Al suffered discrimination in his homeland. They were exemplary parents, citizens, neighbors—the bedrock of their family.

Ray's parents, two sisters, their husbands, aunts, uncles, nieces and nephews (a boatload of relatives) comprised the group. Being part of a huge, cohesive clan was a new, not entirely easy, experience.

Adele was a master chef whose Hungarian dishes, home baked breads and pastries deserved their own books.[85] [86] No one—not drop-in guest or family—ever left hungry.

Ray joined the L.A. District Attorney's office; I returned to graduate school to become a teacher. We'd lived in a succession of charming older duplexes, but finally bought a tract home in San Pedro, overlooking a clutter of roof tops. Soon, we advanced to our dream home which surpassed all expectations. The American dream realized.

If, during marriage, I'd felt something was missing, I kept it to myself. Teacher training addressed the issue: The chance to exercise my mind and skills, too long dormant, provided the sweet opportunity to be useful.

Teaching was, for me, a transcendent way to encourage others, and *express,* in a larger than personal fashion,

85. See Edward O. Thorp, *A Man For All Markets* (New York: Random House, 2017), 55–56, 58–59.
86. Karen L. Thorp, Raun L. Thorp, *From Adele's Kitchen* (Los Angeles, 1989).

the love I felt. For me, to serve others in that fashion was to serve God.

When, in childhood, I'd given my all to something, I'd been drawn "up" into states beyond self. Once again, welling up, was that odd and glorious call I could not, would not, thwart—nor articulate. How to describe the indwelling *agape* love seeking release through what I sensed was a vocation? [87]

These were still the days when wives could not give themselves fully to work outside the home, be it career or calling.[88] I knew I was not made to be a nun, but felt what I imagined was the same fiery passion for some type of superordinate purpose. To the degree my absorption intensified, to that degree our marriage faltered. Repeatedly, I failed to explain what I felt.

How strange that those we love most are so often least likely to hear or understand us. I myself did not grasp the fullness of my aims. For, as it turned out, my goal was God: I was thirsty, and the Spirit said, "Come... take the water of life freely."[89]

How to describe my need to pray, to study, to be undistractedly alone much of the time? How pecuiar, in its biblical sense, to be procured by Another. Slowly, slowly, as novelist Gertrude Stein said, the truth comes out of us. Slowly, slowly came strength to speak, and walk out, my spiritual truth—not without pain.

---

87. *agape* love is the Greek-Christian term for the highest form of love (e.g., compassionate, self-sacrificing love), the sort God has for man and that man has for God.

88. See for e.g., *Mad Men,* 2008, A Lion's Gate TV series (2009) for a picture of the customs of the era.

89. Revelations 22:17

Strange to admit, I felt no longer my own. That seems true of anyone called to contemplative life. Knowing precious little about that then, I just heard the Spirit saying, "Come, follow Me, be radically, necessarily, free."[90]

Rather than be shut down for sharing such tender, sacred, even dangerous nudges, I sought refuge in the soft, "useless," silence of prayer.[91] About these peculiar feelings, I kept still, sensing something would give. My dearest others looked away if I mentioned increasing frustrations. Left unspoken was the obvious: I'd changed. As had the world.

TURMOIL IN THE FIELD

There was so much happening, all around just then. November, 1963: President John F. Kennedy was killed. Two days more: Lee Harvey Oswald, Kennedy's accused assassin, was killed. April, '68: Martin Luther King, Jr. was assassinated. Two months more: Senator Robert Kennedy was killed. Normally I ignored the outer world, yet everyone in America and beyond was caught up in that tumultuous era. In that darkness, I found my way. We all asked, "How might I serve and add value?" The light bulb came on one day at our local laundromat.

As a father and his preschooler put their wash in the dryer and sat by me, the child asked me to read to her from a dog-eared book she'd brought. I read, her dad listened, then asked, "Are you a teacher? You're a natural." His words struck a chord.

Ultimately, as noted, a teacher's training course at Cal State helped me fall in love—but not in a carnal way.

---

90. Corinthians 3:17
91. H. Mehta, "Prayer is Useless," *New York Times*, June 27, 2018.

The ardor, the wholehearted engagement, the sheer excitement that my studies awakened in me was unexpected. I felt as if I'd found a bit of Heaven on earth. I wondered, "What took me so long?"

Educational theory, philosophy, the teaching methods that translated lofty ideas into practical application captivated me. For example, I saw individualized instruction (so meaningful in childhood) as a tangible honoring of each student's inmost gifts. Which all of us are obliged to protect, to nurture.

Student uniqueness, learning pace, interests—genuine enthusiasm for expressing his or her most precious truths—all these, I believed added up to *true* learning: the unfolding identity of who we really are.

The beauty of educational *theory* is seen when teachers meet the needs of students, each one with a distinctive self and learning style. A child's learning intricacies, background, and potential can develop, *if* individualized attention can be provided. When a teacher is dull-witted, rude, fearful, disrespectful, pupils easily reflect that by *not* learning.

In the summer of 1965, just before signing up for student teaching, a mundane traffic citation of a drunk driver erupted into the Watts Riots. Longstanding citizen grievances against police led to widespread burning, looting and violence. The chaos lasted about a week, and directly affected L.A. County schools where I planned to teach.

The upscale Westside of L.A was my expected student teaching location. Immediately changing my plans, I signed up for a federal teacher training program that had announced openings in Watts-Willowbrook. I knew that's where I'd do my student teaching.

Casual contemplatives, more than cloistered, may respond actively to circumstances. Certainly, in youth I did.

As noted earlier, the aim of every true contemplative's life is God. The *way* to God is "charity." [92] That love, events now said I could express through my brand of teaching.

MASTER TEACHERS AS MENTORS

Student teachers spend about two terms in two different Master Teachers' classes. Mrs. Katarina Hargrove (first grade), and Mrs. Winso Starks (seventh grade) were my mentors.[93] Light shone in their classrooms.

These outstanding professionals demonstrated their unique *art* of teaching. They taught, then watched me teach, correcting, guiding, modeling. They checked my lesson plans, meticulously explaining how and why their classroom control was so effective. Two different types of teachers, two different classrooms, yet each with a gentle, child-centered philosophy. Both exuded a prodigious calm. The children loved them. So did I. Their caring example taught me what it means to give one's self away. Here again: transcendent love.

Both disciplined their classes in non-threatening ways. To the disruptive, they'd softly command, "Come here." Typically, the class went quiet; spellbound, waiting for the (expected) adult tirade. They'd no doubt experienced loud, sarcastic or even hostile, reprimands. Instead, these Master Teachers took the child aside and spoke privately until the student nodded, cooperatively returned to his or her seat. We all learned lasting lessons. For me, teaching really is all about love—both gentle *and* tough.

The children grasped the obvious: their classmate's

---

92. Ward, op cit., xv.
93. In Los Angeles, the term "Master Teacher" designates those educators who qualify as capable and equipped temperamentally to train other teachers.

dignity had been preserved. Order was restored without abuse. With this teacher they were safe.

I imagined that some students emulated that sensible way of de-escalating conflict. Standing alongside these teachers during their discussions was a personalized course in teaching and group dynamics. They'd tell a student something like, "I feel you *want* to learn and be helpful to our class, but that it's hard for you to control yourself. Are you willing for us to meet later, just you and me, and work together to solve this?" The collaboration worked; it was real caring, not, I must add, manipulation.

The student, basking in respect and empathy, invariably agreed, tried harder to behave. Repeatedly, I saw that kindly, soft-spoken, personal attention averted problems. Those Master Teachers influenced my whole teaching and leadership style. They proved one could be simply oneself and succeed. It's an understatement that I was highly motivated.

LESSONS AND CONTEMPLATIVE INFLUENCES

Back then, being eager to belong, to fit in, to achieve, I can't honestly say I gave God much consideration. Yes, I prayed, but still never discussed my spiritual life with anyone. That pattern persisted until my late-twenties.

If high school and college taught me anything, it was that I loved to work, to be of service, and to figure things out on my own. Whether learning to navigate U.C.L.A.'s huge campus, or drive, or buy a car, or pass multiple-choice quizzes (barely), challenges were engrossing. Was it possible, at times, for externals to accommodate me? I wasn't sure how that happened, but thought that this involved ultimate Reality, the interplay between strong faith—the Abraham variety which, assuredly, begins with God's conception and our faith, or intent in consciousness. This was private research, and thrilling. In years to come, I named that supernal adjustment *creative* adaptation, a kind of sympathetic action between Heaven and earth.[94] The notion occupies me to this day.[95] Nothing, and no one, had yet invited me to discuss spiritual ideas; so my biggest concern was *how* to express the urgency and excitement of my inner odyssey.

Called as I later was to "live in exile" (i.e., set apart, but not cloistered), a flexible discipline came in handy. It's still helpful. Like most contemplatives, now I'll start each day with a "morning watch"—prayers, meditation, Scripture and related study. The practice turns mind and heart to God. The balance of my time, with periodic breaks, is spent on home and professional affairs. Evenings involve more prayer, meditation, study, and Netflix.

Those long walks alone in high school trained my meditative mind. Which pictured how I'd spend time if given my druthers. The older and more confident I grew, the easier it was to be simply myself—a holy ambition, as straight-forward as carpentry; as sacred as Creation itself. Here, I credit my old friend Paul, and my Master Teachers for being so direct. They reinforced my desire to be just who I am whether alone, or with others. My learning principle? Let's watch someone *being and doing* what we hope to be and do.

AN ADDED GRACE

I began keeping notes for imagined books. Writing let me express what my social sphere disallowed. Articles on

---

94. Here, *The Lord's Prayer's* last two lines fit: "...they will be done in earth as it is in heaven." (KJV)
95. See: Marsha Sinetar, *Living Happily Ever After* (New York: Villard/Random House), 1990.

leadership came first. There was *so* much I wanted to say. What was spiritually most compelling (to me) would be, I felt, valuable to readers. Truth like that, in mystic Meister Eckhart's terms, is the Fire that changes everything into Itself. I didn't know it then, but *I* was the one being changed, translated into the Kingdom of Light.[96]

Old ordeals enabled me to teach, guide, and protect children—and the child in the adults with whom I'd later work. All those fears and losses now served a higher purpose. Trials equipped me to *speak* my heart, to talk in words others understood about, say, the transformative power of suffering. I spoke without religious buzz-words. Similarly, students taught *me* about myself, showed me who they were, what they needed, and how to support and even set firm limits for them. That's how teaching developed me, my skills, and a vision of some larger life. No minor grace. I thank God for it.

Learning as fast and as much as possible from every source, I wanted students to receive whatever might enrich their whole life, not just grades. That South Central assignment introduced me to a new depth of service. It radiated to students, then parents, until the whole community seemed a *living*, learning "organism." After a year such ideas (and my temperament) proved unsuitable for the County's bureaucratic protocols. Administrative policies, in my opinion, were unbelievably controlling, inflexible, micromanaging. I found another, much smaller, truly outstanding district—a perfect pairing.

Torrance Unified became my professional home for the next decade. Initially, I taught third grade, then—

---

96. Collossians 1:13

suddenly—was reassigned to seventh and eighth grade English. Thanks to my Master Teachers, I survived.

The principal, Dr. Ralph Wilson, was a formidable educator. He, too, became my mentor. He appointed me to local and state committees, campaigning for my becoming a principal in record time. Before that, I was made a Master Teacher. I flourished professionally because of Dr. Wilson's support. Around then, I earned my Master's in Public Administration, confident that I'd add value to a school in some leadership spot. As in childhood, my focus on what I loved was not uniformly well-received.

For over a decade, Ray and I had been content together. By the late seventies, that changed. We lived in different worlds, had different world-views. It's said that a happy marriage asks each one to look with the other in the *same* direction. That, we could no longer do.

Raymond J. Sinetar

&

Chapter 8

OF BRIGHT AND FRUITFUL THINGS

I feel sure that if you were here to see how happy I am...you could not call me away...[or] think of calling me to make machines or a home, or of rubbing me against other minds, or of setting me up for measurement. —**John Muir** [97]

The principalship was the best "job" I'd ever had. Here was a chance for real influence: Hiring, setting of goals and objectives, supervision, evaluation of teacher performance. One had a staff, a budget, ancillary support (e.g., nurse, psychologist, custodian, art and music teachers). All of it expanded my vision of what a school could be, what a motivated team could accomplish. Judy Williams was a top-notch secretary. Her mature sense of propriety *and* whimsy made us a high-trust team; lasting friends.

Even in my first year, innovative ideas flowed. When these were sound—say, in individualized instruction—we went for it. Repeatedly, the district supervisor cautioned, "Marsha, don't be too creative." Repeatedly, the Central Office called me downtown where the Superintendent diplomatically scolded and asked, "What if everyone did that?"

---

97. *John Muir, In His Own Words*, compiled, edited by Peter Browning (LaFayette, CA: Great West Books, 1988), 86-17.

I thought, but never said outright, "Then I'd be nuts not to try it." Our school became known for attempting innovative programs.

For instance, we invited the children to paint a mural on a long outdoor wall. That was the first view people had of our school when entering the grounds. The bright, child-centered images of stick figures, dogs, cats, stars, rainbows reminded visitors that youngsters "lived" there. That happy, lively wall garnered a positive, welcoming response. Much to my supervisors' amazement, the children's drawings and gaiety prompted field trips from other schools. Students took turns as guides, proudly showing off their work. Their parents were ecstatic.

Did management secretly enjoy having a young renegade in their midst? I sensed tacit approval for creativity, feeling like a favored child in that family of exemplary leaders.

Or was that unspoken go-ahead to innovate merely political? Namely, our upscale-area school had strong, vocal community backing. Our parent base had clout.

Our constituency was articulate, well-educated, politically active with the local Board of Education. At PTA and other meetings, I felt waves of support (and, to be sure, a smattering of disapproval) when explaining the learning precepts behind my individualizing methods. I sensed parents knew that I loved their children, as if my own.

I'd found my voice. Inordinate self-consciousness about speaking in public had been debilitating. Now, expressing ideals about educating the *whole* person, I spoke with zeal.

Before long, we became a Demonstration School for the District, and teacher-training colleges like UCLA.

Universities and other school districts visited to observe our individualized methods and other, child-centered programs. Our parent-volunteers were our biggest supporters; they spread the word about some of the techniques we were using.[98]

LINING UP WITH ELTON

Instead of ringing a bell in the morning for students to line up, we played Elton John's *Philadelphia Freedom* over the loudspeaker. First, we'd all meet in class rows on the blacktop. The children (and a few teachers) marched into place in step with the music; some sang along: "Shine the light; Shine the light." Next, we said the Pledge of Allegiance. This, with gusto, inspired by Elton's words. Finally, parents watched, smiling, as their children happily pranced/danced into class. The song mirrored my patriotism about America and motivated me, too. What a rousing, even meditative, start to each day.

Increasingly, I was invited to speak on leadership and educational topics at statewide conferences. That led, first, to consulting for other districts, then to my tiny advisory firm for the private sector. In effect, to paraphrase John Briggs, an authority on creativity, I had experienced the "crystalizing revelation" that *directs* expression of deepest truths about life.[99] So that's how this teacher found, or invented, new forms of education—through dialogue, writing, leadership and communication variants. By con-

---

98. I hope to write a book about our innovative methods, the superior faculty/parent relations, and the exemplary reviews we received when, as an Early Childhood Education school (for the State) we excelled in the independent ratings of the ECE reviewers.
99. John Briggs, *Fire in the Crucible* (Los Angeles, CA: J.P. Tarcher, Inc., 1990), 256.

tributing some useful, heartfelt expressions derived from the inner Kingdom, the problem of finding a life's work was solved.

My spiritual ardor overshadowed life in my creaturely world. At home, I was lost. This happens, not only to contemplatives, but also to many who are growing aware of the highest Source of life. Professionally, I was flourishing. Personally, I was anguished.

GRIEF WORK

Few marriages allow for so profound a shift of focus as mine. Ours did not survive. My way of being played a solid part, but not entirely. Suffice it to say, Ray and I were both at a loss, heart-broken, suffering. I could not—would not—fulfill the conventional wifely role.

Marriage counseling left me tongue-tied. I shut down—felt misunderstood, hopeless. I suspect Ray endured something similar; doubtlessly we each felt more isolated when sitting together over coffee than when alone. A year or more of that misery and we threw in the towel—a shock to his family, although his mother and I somehow moved through it remaining mother-and-daughter-close until she died a decade or more later.

Utter devastation. Life lost meaning. At work, Judy, the most trustworthy secretary, shielded me when, in extreme anguish, I shut my office door to cry. I've always shown emotion freely, but the toll my path now had taken was too steep. In despair, I reminded God that He'd promised not to allow trials greater than we could bear.[100] This

---

100. 1 Cor. 10:13 Biblical translations may use the word "temptation," but "trials"—being put to a test—is also commonly employed in this verse.

was too much. I could not go on. Suddenly, the small, still voice within said, "Just wait."

Before acting on a depressive impulse, I wrote out a vow: to wait seven years before doing anything rash. Then went shopping for a therapist.

And after interviewing a few head-trippers, I was led to Beverly Hills—to "Dr. Saul," a portly, insightful psychiatrist. He was hopeful, witty, bright. Two months, many sessions and tests later he, with twinkling eyes, concluded, "Marsha, you're not sick, just very, very sad."

Saul explained: Because I'd never fully *felt* my father's death, *delayed grief* had set in. Divorce, another type of death, accentuated my sorrow. To survive—to support myself, then heed a calling—I'd buried old and current losses. As Dr. Saul said, "One way or another, emotions speak." Mine spoke through tears and tenacious heartache.

Saul insisted that life involves finding ways to shoulder at least some suffering. Each manages that differently. He added, "So now we work."

Therapy seemed like a graduate course in dealing with the distresses of ordinary life. In effect, "adjustment" didn't mean that everyday problems vanish; if we're emotionally healthy, we simply learn, as Abraham Maslow once wrote, how and when to step back, rest, nurse our wounds, and gather strength to get on with the business of living.

I worked with Saul and then with his associate ("Dr. Gene") in both group and individual sessions. Things started looking up.

Not all therapists are equally able. Our group was blessed to be focused on effectiveness, rather than symptoms of learned helplessness. No victimization. We examined counter-productive attitudes and choices, comparing these to options that worked. If, for instance, someone sank into a sea of self-blame, Gene might offer examples that illustrated how selfish and unselfish drives *fuse* in high functioning, creative people. Since most of us were in the arts or leadership positions, his emphasis on creativity had strong appeal.

A SECOND, MORE CAREFREE CHILDHOOD?

Our group was lively, social, homogeneous. We were an enterprising, high-achieving lot, with executive and even celebrity success. We had one mega-star and one famous designer in that group of ten or so. It was fun.

We listened to, kidded (and confronted) each other when someone postured, minimized flaws, or hogged the "sharing" stage. We cried and laughed our way to higher spirits, realizing repeatedly that, in our human condition, we all agonize once in a while.

Typically, after "group," we'd go out for dinner or dancing, this being the age of disco. Soon, a new phase of hilarious friends and free-wheeling antics dominated my leisure hours. Now cane relief, a release after the discipline and industry of the past. I confess to a dissolute spree.

After each day's work as a principal, my new pals and I went nightclubbing until near dawn. This was the adolescence I'd not really known. That sowing of wild oats continued for about a year. Oh yes, there were misadventures (including a second, four-month marriage). At the end of that low point of self-indulgence, a month's stay in Malibu with Carol—my college roommate—brought me to my senses. Carol's sunny, sensible friendship restored normalcy. I didn't feel guilty; more like, "Thanks. I needed that."

Surprisingly, there were benefits to loosening the reins of what had been a somewhat up-tight manner. The more I'd relaxed, the more relational success rolled in; especially at work where all was bright.

Invitations poured in to speak about leadership at other districts, and corporate conferences. Our school tripled in volunteers. Just as my family's good times had been light-hearted, so was our campus a jolly place to be. And yet, serious learning took place.

I'd ended therapy, and begun a Ph.D. program. Dr. Gene's parting advice: Given my temperament, a spiritual discipline like meditation might be in order. That idea felt right, as if I'd known that was in my future.

DÉJÀ VU DAYS

Lengthy, intensive research into diverse disciplines followed: Transcendental Meditation, Zen, Centering prayer, and weekly visits to a wide range of Christian churches. I'd met these ideas before. This was somehow more stimulating and right. After learning many different meditation methods I returned to my own, intuitively-inspired program. Forty years later, I still devote time daily to that discipline of "listening inwardly," contemplative prayer, study of Scripture. [101]

At a Charismatic Evangelical church, I spoke in tongues, (still do when in deep prayer). During a Quaker Meeting, I experienced the Presence behind my right side. Not since childhood had I been so profoundly touched.

---

101. See 1 Samuel 3:9, "Speak, Lord, for your servant hears." *That's* inward listening.

Like most with a mystical bent, such conversion experiences came anytime—while meditating or praying; while taking walks, or chopping onions. The most consequential one occurred suddenly as I drove to work.

Cruising along Pacific Coast Highway in my blue Honda Civic, I was enjoying a glassy, steel gray sea. Abruptly, dazzling white light infused my entire being—hands, arms, innards—and my car, the ocean, the road. *Everything* within and without was soaked in Light, *was* Light. Having entered the fullness of Christ, I'd been raised up, over the shadow of this world, beyond surface appearances, into the true nature of things, Reality. In a moment, all returned to normal. Except me.

The veil that the mystics describe had lifted. In poet John Gillespie Magee, Jr.'s words, I had "slipped the surly bonds of earth…and touched the face of God." [102] Everyday forms were not as I'd assumed; even others seemed an illusion.[103] How clear that, with (or "in") the Mind of Christ, we understand that cryptic precept: God (Light) appeared in the world as flesh.[104]

For a moment I had no longer inhabited a dusty, sensory world. I was part of One Being, the living Spirit—some will say "Universes"—completely still, illumined. Immediately, came indescribable contrition, deep regret for my fall from childhood's simpler, faithful heart and inherited Grace.[105]

---

102. His poem, "High Flight", is in the public domain.
103. Matthew 4:16 and at least twenty other biblical passages refer to that light, but most interpret that in figurative terms.
104. 1st Timothy 3:16 (KJV)
105. Psalm 16:5,6.

The following Sunday, I requested baptism in a pictur-esque Anglican church in El Segundo. That outer, most healing act amidst a gathering of unknowns marked my inner allegiance to a new Family.

After which, my true self showed up—unhurriedly—as a progressive *life's* unfolding. This was no quick-fix. As Ephesians 2 puts it, I was still afar off, still conversing with the lusts of the flesh. However, the next years brought an increasing faith, through grace. I began to "know the love of Christ that passes knowledge" that I might be filled with the fullness of God. [106].

This has been more a *finding* than a seeking; a kind of mutual, double-edged entry into the divine love. I felt I was relocating into the Household of God in a practical, speak-your-mind, pay-your-bills, contributive way of being amongst others. Yet I was drawn increasingly into a vast stillness.

A primitive, mystical poem elaborates:

> The Soul says, "I would be saved," while
> jointly Christ says, "I would save."[107]

All such hearing happens, as philosopher Max Picard reminds us, in the Silence that is a *Presence* uttering Itself into us when thought and language cease. Silence in soli-tude was now a needful state—no, *not* isolation, as if imprisoned in a jail cell—but, for me, the vital precursor to real love, and liberty, real giving.[108]

The next decade seemed riddled with the small deaths that lead to larger life.[109] It took *years* to give up my wish

---

106. Ephesians 2; 3: 19
107. Evelyn Underhill, *Mysticism*, p. 134.
108. Max Picard, *The World of Silence* (South Bend, IN: Regenery/Gateway, Inc., 1952).
109. Colossians 3:2

to please others, and to say, "No," to pointless activities without guilt. True freedom.[110]

Soon, I felt like the "odd man out." Normal socializing became tedious, often unbearable. Paradoxically, service-oriented interactions sustained me— for instance, when in a real dialogue or focused on others' needs. While I crept toward the renewal of habits described in monastic literature, my dear ones thought me absurd. Only someone with a deep religious impulse who lives amidst scoffers will understand.

Ignoring the tone of disapproval in others' voices, I sold the first home I'd bought on my own, relocated to an old, woodsy farmhouse up north, certain that Christ's "sell all and follow Me" dictum was in line with these actions. It wasn't easy. I craved my family's approval. Yet, I stepped out, felt braver. And rural life in the redwoods strengthened courage. John Muir's words rang true: "Fears vanish as soon as one is fairly free in the wilderness." [111]

Since I wasn't called to a formal cloister, I created my own "all-American" version of contemplative life. Hadn't I cultivated the ingenious ways and means of my adopted country? To me, being "American" meant freedom to pursue life in a contributive, if also resourceful fashion.

So it happened that, over my forties and ever more with age, I shaped an unorthodox life—unmarried, uncoupled, unconventionally worshipful—while living in a rustic community, "hid with Christ in God."[112] Thereby, could I give as richly as possible to the good of others in

---

110. John 8:35
111. Ibid, 60-272
112. Colossians 3:3

ways meant for me. Supporting family and corporate life from an "outsider's" stance, enhances my usefulness. That, too, is vocation.

In the natural, I had no road map. Study, *learning* from all manner of denominations invited knowledge of the divine will. The rapt attention of my religious investigations opened a door to deeper prayer. Each day I'd harness anxiety. How to arrange quieter things when so naturally outgoing? I envisioned a solitary life, with my soul redirected to things above, but I needed a single-mindedness born of relationship with God. I was hindered by caring that those I admired thought me odd and "selfish" for craving a life set apart. How to outgrow this?

One day Job 23:14 spoke to me: "*...He performeth the thing that is appointed for me...*" I'd been leaning on my own powers. So came another, slow shift of mind, mostly during contemplative prayer.

Insights moved thought down memory lane. Images of coming to the U.S. swirled around in my mind.

Since girlhood, I'd admired the bold ingenuity, the melding of cultures so integral to the American ethos. So what if I wasn't well-suited for monastic life?

Then struck the lightening bolt: Wasn't I living in the Land of the Free? America seemed built on a *spiritual* idea: Everything lawful is allowed.[113] Much self-examination followed. Why bow down to what others thought? Why not shape and arrange my own, informal contemplative life? Why couldn't one serve God and neighbor in one's self-styled, solitary (if casual) fashion? Answers forced slow, deliberate change.

---

113. See 1 Cor. 6 12-20—(not usually interpreted as I am doing here, but still...).

MY PATTERN FOR POSITIVE ACTION[114]

Ancient monks infused me with their blueprint of life. They'd had a burning, *focused* desire for union with God. That wasn't merely wishful thinking, not just "a dream." They'd turned their entire lives around to actualize the living Christ within. Since that was my goal, they became my "best case" models—my private, if distant, mentors.[115] From these spiritual identifications emerged a concrete vision of writing *as* teaching. Many of my early books flowed out of these passionate years.

Then, too, my distant mentors took risks. Why couldn't I? First came time-off from work. Two unpaid sabbaticals later, during which I earned a Ph.D. in psychology, I left the public sector, formed my own leadership firm, and moved northward to an unpopulated area. Before that, during my final sabbatical, I conducted my brand of unique research.

Wondering if and how I'd survive a business failure, or tolerate the loss-of-face, funds, a much-loved occupation, and I wanted a sturdy financial base for my new life, I first chose to test myself.[116]

The divine spark that prompts our boldest moves was urging me on. To triumph over the spiritual slavery of fear, a critical assessment seemed in order. Freedom was not license to do whatever I wanted.[117] Reasoning that without learning what's achievable there's no growth, ultimately I inched into unknowns; that helped balance fear and the

---

114. In my *Developing a 21st Century Mind,* I discussed the value of productive prototypes in one's strategic planning process.

115. Marsha Sinetar, *The Mentor's Spirit* (New York: St. Martin's Press).

116. Luke 6: 46-49 speaks to this point: A solid foundation is required, whether building a house, a business, or chosing our way of life.

117. Thomas Merton speaks eloquently of this in *The New Man,* Farrar, Straus, & Giroux, New York, 1961.

urge to grow. Research—information—was essential. How would I fare if my little firm tanked? After all, I planned to quit a hard-won, ultra-secure position, invest my paltry pension funds in a high-wire entrepreneurial scheme. No easy venture for one still smarting from the financial privations of youth. A fun experiment came to mind as I meandered northward, working and living in L.A. traveling around the country for business, scouting new home areas, when possible.

"MAY I TAKE YOUR ORDER?"

Bernie, the owner of a Malibu deli, asked if I'd waitressed before. "No," said I, "but I can cook, clean, and love people." Hired.

Waiting tables is hard work. Being unknown was easy, refreshing—an adventure. No one at the deli asked (or cared) about college degrees or one's past. You could create yourself. My co-workers (mostly actors) were happy to have a flexible work schedule. As was I.

On Saturdays and Sundays, I waited tables, scrubbed grills and freezer racks. Monday through Friday, I had a day job developing curriculum for the District and instructing principals on its implementation. Late afternoons and some evenings were devoted to free-lancing as an advisor to senior managers in private-sector firms.

Anonymity had its charms. At the deli, I practiced the edict in Galatians 5:13, to "...serve one another in love." The lesson? To the degree one serves one's neighbor, one serves God. Here came true fulfillment. As noted, in the climate of that Love, so does our desert bloom. The Buddhist notion of "mindfulness" also worked: simple, caring, *conscious usefulness* seems a universal key to success. Attending to orders, cleaning up meticulously, remembering names is not just emotionally profitable. It pays off monetarily. My tips from customers proved the point.

Eureka! I discovered that "I" could earn a living no matter what. Serving others in the Spirit of Love was the secret to supply. Yes, it's best when our function utilizes some inborn talent, but posh jobs and titles are not soul-satisfying. Not for me anyway. What a breakthrough.

With that, I quit waitressing, quit my tenured position, and created Sinetar & Associates—my party of one (there were no associates). Within two weeks, that little firm was financially solvent

COLD CALLING AND CORPORATE FELLOWSHIP

Dr. Frank Michaelson, head of Human Resources for Dart Industries, was one of the first to retain my solo outfit. He'd responded favorably to my cold call. These unsolicited phone overtures aimed to set up meetings at which I'd describe my firm's services. By the end of week two, I'd secured three appointments, Frank being one. As he remarked, "Kid, you can sell!"

I'd phoned numerous unknown corporations to arrange exploratory conversations, in person. Dart Industries was one of L.A.'s Fortune 500 companies. Unbeknownst to me, Dart was entering an era of mergers and acquisitions. My skills dovetailed with upper management's need for corporate training and development. The leadership piece of mergers and acquisitions (a.k.a., M & A and change-management) became my area of expertise; methods I'd used to foster a learning climate in schools applied. Who knew God's mysterious ways might embrace the cold calling that resulted in such synchrony? (Good things typically follow our first steps, if taken in faith.)

Frank and I hit it off, having much in common besides business. We were both John le Carré fans. Each of us repeatedly re-read *all* of le Carré's books, strongly resonating with George Smiley—le Carré's inscrutable British intelligence officer. Smiley's private, reflective life appealed to us, as doubtlessly it did to most high-ranking, organizational types and/or secular contemplatives. Anyone in responsible roles, handling sensitive, close-to-the-vest issues seems, like Smiley, a double-agent. Frequently, le Carré, and some of W.E.B. Griffin's military characters, mentored my navigations through the currents of corporate waters.

Then, too, our backgrounds were alike. Frank had traveled in Asia, was an educator with a Ph.D. in psychology. As a retired officer, like many Dart executives, his work ethic was much like the one I'd so admired in my dad: Task and achievement oriented, focused, more observant than talkative.

WORK AS A SPIRITUAL PATH

My signature method involved *dialogue:* What that splendid author and Cistercian monk, Thomas Merton, called *"an exchange of selves."* Whether in group or individual meetings, my presentations typically encouraged a time of open discussion.

These personalized sessions were true agents of change, if also conducted for different purposes. Topics and challenges changed. My *process* didn't. An amiable exchange was our norm. It built trust—the essential glue for organizations in flux.[118]

---

118. For more benefits of dialogue, see Marsha Sinetar, "The Informal Discussion Group—Powerful Agent for Change", M.I.T., *Sloan Management Review*, 1988.

The trickiest behavior for my clients was dropping the tightly-scripted posture that most companies expect of executives. Parroting the "party line" tends to be the kiss of death to sound relationships. By contrast, properly facilitated dialogue groups can build common ground. For that result, an informal give-and-take works wonders.

I mention Dart Industries because its senior team was the first corporation to give me free rein to innovate. No question but that freedom has always been a necessity for my best ideas. Which may explain why lucrative contracts with constricting legal clauses have been stumbling blocks. Whenever I've coaxed myself into one of these agreements, I've lived to regret it. Inspired ideas

At a book signing

tend to wither and die if held captive to inflexible, micro-managing dictates. Ever since then, knowing on which side my bread is buttered I've avoided rigid contractual set ups.

Years of corporate work ushered in years of creative output: I drew and exhibited pen-and-ink art and etchings, and illustrated my book covers. I became engrossed with real estate, while simultaneously writing.

Although we're often advised to write about what we know, I wrote to uncover what I didn't yet understand. On fire to tell of a growing faith in Spirit-led, contemplative practices, I was emboldened and labored nonstop. Every capacity, invested wisely, birthed new, unexpected talent. Eacn one from above, not below.

CONTEMPLATIVE INFLUENCES

Around this time, notions such as the Benedictine's *"pray and work"* began to exert a strong pull. I considered my work—regardless of its form—as a ministry of sorts, although back then I was *far* removed from any such admission.

Recently a remark by Professor Arthur Brooks struck me as befitting any contemplative, informal or precise:

> [Our] secular vocations are actually priestly vocations, and [we] have an opportunity to bring people, in the newest sense, to the oldest traditions.[119]

Upbringing, life abroad, years devoted to both private and public sector involvements have shaped my religious

---

119. Arthur C. Brooks, Professor of Public Leadership, Harvard-Kennedy College has posted the above idea on his YouTube talk titled *Love Your Enemies*.

views and language. My father's vibrant work ethic lingers as a natural impulse. Disposition inclines me to silence and solitude, yet some type of interactive service feels essential—like breathing. Experience has trained me to connect with people from every walk. Could that explain the "crossover" language that appears in my book?

Back then, I needed a conciliatory vocabulary for my divinely inspired worldview. Feeling that almost everyone thirsted for their life's animating essence, I wove religious threads and paraphrased stories into every possible application. The toughest, most hide-bound clients resonated with the universality of these ancient ideals.

My first books spoke of monks, mystics, of work as devotion; of healing choices, spiritually precocious children, even of films. I was teaching, perhaps encouraging, readers to consider prayer, meditation, the power of intention, and attention to issues "above and not below," focused on spiritual, not worldly, issues—as I am doing still. Rejection letters could paper the walls. (It took ten years for Do What You Love...to get published.) Continually, I war against discouragement. This, "...that I might win those under the law."[120]

Further, to understand my ideas, no student or client needed to leave their church, join a new movement, or feel defensive about the doctrines of their own faith. Since every culture has its contemplative arm, it seemed enough to say "This is how I see things, but you phrase such matters in your way, in your heart's terms."

---

120. 1 Corinthians 9:19-20

SPIRITUAL SOLITUDE *AS* RELATIONSHIP

Again: The spiritual solitary is not isolated. True contemplatives (aka: mystics) "practice" God's Presence.[121] One simply brings the divine love (or Christ, or the Holy Spirit, etc.) into awareness. Which can be so captivating as to make superficial socializing an irritant—the distraction that disrupts our peace. [122] We're engaged with what I've heard called "the business of all business." Yes, we may experience a "dark night of the soul," but as Thomas Merton points out somewhere or other, usually that's merely the drama of our narcissistic self. Solitude and silence are requirements of the soul's ascent to her highest plane of life. It's that seamless blending of self and God, or the here-and-now realization of Truth in our inward parts.[123]

Contemplative solitude means living for and with the inner man of the heart. This was my lot. With one, highly interactive exception: Work. Whether with children, parents, clients, eventually graduate students, and writing, a self-forgetful service became essential. That was my outlet for the spirituality that requires usefulness, productive engagement. Even the monk or nun in a cell prays for others, not simply (perhaps rarely) for self. A phrase that fits is "Love in action."[124]

Sure enough, clarity came during both the most profound moments of prayer and the most productive teach-

---

121. See Brother Lawrence, *The Practice of the Presence of God* (New York: Simon & Schuster).

122. See Exodus 33:13, 11.

123. Psalm 51:6

124. *Agape love:* The highest form of love (charity), transcends the usual familial, romantic, and carnal bonds.

ing, advisory, or creativity efforts; the latter, even when lecturing or counseling another. Concentrating fully on another raises the mind to infinite fields of answers, all knowledge. In that inner silence, I'd realize that to be "set apart" merely adjusts the form of daily life or relationships.

The quality of each form depends on the degree of accord, attention, commitment to and with what's sacred, most loved and meaningful. Service, caring, contribution, fruitfulness—these are made more loving, if and as I turn body, mind, soul to God.

LESSONS AND CONTEMPLATIVE INFLUENCES

Time spent in contemplative fashion was—is—the seed bearing fruit of its own kind. No scholastic degree, no "head-tripping" talk raises me up in stillness. Only "the crown and summit" of a tranquil mind at prayer prepares me for time spent elsewhere.[125] That's my influence now.

Take interactions with others: In my "dialogue sessions," to the extent One encounters the God-Who-is-here,[126] One senses growth, learning, insight, as the living Truth envelops us.

So comes the reciprocity of real connection wherein two become One.[127] For a split second there is no separation. Almost any work done in this unitive way invites the *teleios*—completion—of one's very being. From glad silence, from the Holy Wilderness, comes my place in the grand scheme of things. Yet it's often wordless.

---

125. This is how one monk, Father J. Borst, described contemplative prayer, wherein we don't look for results, but simply rest in God's presence.
126. Abhishiktananda, *Prayer* (Kashmir, Delhi: ISPCK), 57.
127. Deuteronomy 6:4

Teaching, writing, being in dialogue with people–
these absorb me totally. And quicken the *shalom* or harmony[128] at my ground of being– that deepest sense that
"all is well with my soul." As noted earlier, the French
monk Abhishiktananda believed that during these times,
when we give out that which is best and noblest in us from
what God has given to us, we become a kind of tithe, a
sacrifice of first fruits.

What a paradox: Solitude and silence reconstitute and
teach me how to give myself to others so that we both are
"fitly framed together," united somehow through the
Spirit, "in a habitation of God."[129] God's grace emerges as
we abide in the Silence that *is*.

These days, so late in life, when sensing myself serving
someone's essential self, or even offering up this meager bit
to the divine purpose, I feel the warmth of rightness, as if,

"Ah, so this is why I was born."

෴

---

128. *Shalom*, a Hebrew word, used in both greeting or departure; it means many
good things (as in a blessing), such as harmony, completeness, wholeness, tranquility, and more.
129. Ephesians 2: 21-22

My mother and brother
in New York ~ circa 1947

My mother and brother
in Santa Fe ~ circa 2000.

AFTERWORD

Later, I will go out into the desert. You can see the stars. You can feel God here. There's a closeness here... It resets me.
—Art Bell [130]

A wonderful thing happened for my mother: She got well. During my marriage, she'd lived on and off with her sister, my Aunt Jeanne. After Uncle Jack died, the two lived together permanently. Supposedly, my mom was my aunt's companion; to me, it was as if the two looked after each other

There was nothing conventional about either; each sister was bright, highly spiritual, expressive. Jeanne displayed bursts of creative energy. She wasn't just a genius home chef, she had unexpected flair in other ways. Once, perhaps around her menopause, she got an impulse to paint her entire kitchen herself. From that day forth, her fridge, stove, and cabinets were baby pink, with gold-flocking. Not quite *Architectural Digest,* but very "her."

My mother had "second sight" (i.e., clairvoyance).[131] As mentioned, she met the shadings of her inner world primarily through the arts, music, *beauty*—in any field. I felt that these sisters emerged from their Middle Eastern, male-dominated upbringing, with "New Age" minds. Their openness to fresh ideas was unrivaled.

---

130. Art Bell, *Somewhere in Time,* Radio show, Premier Network-Coast-to-Coast Radio, rebroadcast of 9/14/19. (Paraphrased remarks of Bell at the end of a difficult broadcast.)
131. As described in my *Dreams unto Holiness.*

Jeanne's positive influence on my mom involved religion of a universal sort. For instance, my aunt was a devotee of three powerful leaders: Bishop Fulton Sheen, evangelist Katherine Kuhlman, *and* founder of Christian Science, Mary Baker Eddy. More dissimilar preachers you'd never find. The common thread? The *healing* actuality of unwavering faith in God.

My mother was amenable to such ideas, particularly to the way explained by Christian Science, later Science of Mind.

Various practitioners of various faiths came calling, provided prayer, spiritual counseling, and healing "treatments." Gradually, my mother's awareness expanded. A regeneration took place. Something healthy, clearer, calmer worked its way into her being. Her core outlook and responses to normal stress improved. Observing this reinforced my bias that God speaks to each soul in an infinitely individualized language, perhaps spoken only to and by the inner man of the heart. We all grasp the Ineffable differently in order that we might be translated out of the power of darkness into the kingdom of God's dear Son.[132] Like when actor George Burns says, in the film *Oh God!,*

"I chose a look you could understand." [133]

Spiritual insight, not drugs, not psychiatric probing, led my mother away from her past extreme situation—whatever that may have been—into a balanced state of mind.

---

132. Colossians 1: 13-14

133. Cited in my book, *Reel Power. Spiritual Growth through Films,* originally published by Ligouri/Triumph in 1997.

She became direct, down-to-earth. Phantoms lost the grip they'd had on her psyche. For the rest of her life my mom remained on an even keel. Who dares say that prayers aren't answered?

In their eighties, the two sisters seemed in fine form. They had fun together. They took tour buses to Las Vegas, returned exuberant about lavish buffets, Liberace or Wayne Newton shows, and small gains at slot machines. When Jeanne passed away, her sons helped my mom find a small apartment, and later assisted living arrangements. Since I then lived in Chicago, their kindness was invaluable.

Work had let me set up a modest trust fund for my mom. She never needed to *ask* for money. A check arrived every month without fail. At last, she was independent, realizing its power. She managed her own budget, checking account, and household affairs. No small victory for a near nonagenarian who'd never done any of that before.

Occasionally, she flew to New Mexico where Anthony had settled. The two remained close throughout their days. It does me good to know that, ultimately, each found a good measure of peace.

As for us—my mother and me, also Anthony—somewhere along the way we discussed the tribulations of our family, agreeing (in tears) that despite the messiness of our relationship, we'd long ago (perhaps before the beginning) forgiven each other, and that we were rooted in the sweet soil of an eternal love.[134] Through it all, God was at work.

---

134. See Chapter 10, M. Sinetar, *Spiritual Intelligence* (Maryknoll, NY: Orbis Books, 2000). I have discussed the eternal nature of forgiveness, and told more of my own childhood. Also, Thomas Merton, whose ideas strongly influence me, also discusses this sort of forgiveness in many of his books.

Without making a huge big deal of it, my mother and brother came to accept my solitary nature. As for my baptism into the Christian faith, my mom's gentle advice? "Just don't take it too seriously." (No doubt spoken by one who'd suffered an "extreme situation" at the hands of ultra-authoritarians—maybe at home, at a long-ago convent, from a cultural mind-set. Water under the bridge.

My ever-prescient mother must have sensed her exit. A few weeks *after* she passed, someone found and sent me a note she'd written, stamped, and put aside for me. Dated just days before she'd passed, her note read:

> *"I love you forever.*
> *Mumy."*

FROM WEAKNESS, STRENGTH

Following our divorce, Ray and I developed a rare friendship. Admittedly, that took time. He'd formed a lasting relationship with a bright, lovely lawyer, Saundra Tonsager Brewer. We, too, became friends. I love and admire the brave, strong, tender Saundra. Today, I'd call her "family," and truly hope that feeling is mutual.

Nearly a decade after I relocated, Ray and Saundra moved into the same community. Our initial, infrequent visits felt awkward. All that changed when it was thought I might lose my eyesight.

While in Chicago, riding in an elevator, I realized I could not see the control buttons. Ophthalmologists diagnosed an anomaly at the back of my eyes. Cause unknown. Perhaps an old accident? Severe near-sightedness? In short, a mystery. Prognosis? Dim.

Panic, then depression set in; the latter came and went. My faithless snake-brain whispered of calamity—mostly at three A.M.; I'd awaken out of a choppy sleep, envisioning the worst. Characteristically, I told only those with a "need to know'" about my eyesight.

Not wishing to talk "the problem," I kept the matter to myself, clinging to the assurance of Hebrews 11: Things still unseen, yet hoped for, exist in and as the *substance* of strong faith.[135] American evangelist Dr. David Jeramiah once spoke of such times as "disruptive seasons." That, it surely was. Some days found me weary; other days, confident. Could I keep my faith, or would I crumble? I wasn't sure.

Never one to ask for anything, now I had no choice. Forced to give up work, travel, and of course, a favorite—driving—I needed help.

Enter Ray. He drove me to doctors, and fulfilled my Costco lists. Saundra became a sister who empathized and supported Ray's noble gestures. How to express thanks to those who want none?

It was tough to be on the receiving end of such largess. So much more agreeable for Pride to give than to receive. In gratitude, I cooked vats of homemade chicken soup for Ray and Saundra. Ray brusquely said it was "too much." Instead, I sent wine (which seemed to satisfy).

PRAYER: MY FIRST AND ONLY OPTION

The medicos offered no anwers. I'd have grasped at any straw since both reading and writing, always so fluid, so effortless, so *essential* had become laborious. Whereas before, I'd written a book a year (while traveling, lecturing, vacationing), now producing a single typo-laden page was a Herculean task, the frustration massive. Three and more

---

135. Hebrews 11:1-2

books a week had been my reading norm; now I'd *try* to read a single sentence, but failing, burst out crying. Five years of such doings, then—on that black night of loss, fear, suffering—a sunlit ribbon of hope. Within me something said, " Rise up above the appearance of even this. Each crushing blow can bring greater strength, and the deeper understanding that bears good spiritual fruit."[136] To the doctors' surprise, the scars began dissolving, micro-molecule, by micro-cell. To this day, improvement continues.

Indeed, I could not have written this book without that massive healing. No, not complete. But it is steady. It is wonderful. I am grateful for it.

Oddly, even before that upturn, beneath a veneer of gloom, a familiar, if inexplicable cheer lifted my spirits. Here came the thought, "There's more to do, much more I can and need to do." Against all hope, fresh hope arrived. With renewed vigor, I began writing again—first, short monographs, then books. How easy to love God and have faith when things go well. How much more grace is received when doing that in anguish.

A crucial realization fell into place: The worst conditions can build faith and "through our weakness" increase God's glorious *spiritual* power—ability to endure, to run the race (if haltingly) we feel born to run. All this, by grace alone, as the following illustration proves.

THE GIFT OF GIFTS

Ray was not a religious man. Typically, he'd stare off into space impatiently if I mentioned God. He never suffered fools. Still, for me, he became a living letter of com-

---

136. John 14; John 12: 24

passion, "written not with ink, but with the Spirit...and read ...by the heart." [137] Here streamed selflessness— *agape* love.[138] To clarify: I did not so much feel love; he could be frosty, stern, reproachful. Rather, I sensed love shining *through* him. It was the exact quality I'd known in my father, my mom when she was well, in my grandmother and Madame; in Kent (my former headmaster); in my Master Teachers, in six year olds and corporate executives —sensed flowing out of so many who've touched my life.

What a marvel that those trials and tests, those friends and neighbors proved that the God-kind-of-love speaks through everything, everyone—even (often especially) "non-believers." I don't say others always express love; only that it reflects *out of* them. And how amazing that the rich, mixed bag of wonders that makes up my days enables love alone to last. Despite the mess and muddle of relationships, after all is said and done, life melts into a great big gift of grace, the pure love that at heart, we *are*.

For here's the secret in all such gifts: the Giver *is* the Gift.

Love will out, must out, however harshly, kindly, or oddly expressed. The divine love shines on all.[139] Whether all receive it is another matter. To miss out on that, is to miss tasting of the entire enchilada of existence.

Such lessons coaxed me to let go of former things. Forgetting what I couldn't do, I tackled whatever I *could*.

---

137. 2 Cor. 3:2-3
138. According to W.E. Vinces, a biblical scholar, the exercise of this sort of love is one of the means God uses to develop likeness to Christ.
139. Titus 2: 11

And walked a much narrower path. Something within sang, "Behold! I will do a new thing." [140]

That's how I started over, almost from "scratch"—along heartfelt vocational lines. I began writing again with a new voice; first, as mentioned, monographs, then smaller, more spiritual books. It was upsettingly slow, but with the sense that I was pouring myself out for the Lord. I recorded CD messages for a varied, spiritually maturing audience (i.e., priests, pastors, and others of that ilk). And reinstated my dialogue sessions, mentoring clients by phone. Once more I learned that if I could hold on in the tough times, a certain inner strengthening brings renewal. [141]

More than ever, I'm convinced that God uses *us* as the *type* of persons we are—warts and all—, and uses every situation, to impart Himself to all Creation. Anyway, that's how I see things as I sit here reminiscing, in my old creaky house.

Nearing eighty, I'm a bit creaky, too, but still writing books, teaching in my way—through recordings, dialogue sessions, and the occasional YouTube video. I walk daily, dust shelves, do laundry, cook up a storm.

Even this far into the game, my inner "Martha" and "Mary" are often at odds, still learning to cooperate. The contemplative Mary's in charge, but my earth-bound Martha continually bugs me about chores—filing papers, answering mail, organizing my affairs. "Stop daydreaming," she complains., "Stop wasting time." Thankfully, I hear Jesus's rebuke:

---

140. Isaiah 43:19
141. 2 Corinthians 4: 16-2

"Ah, Martha, Martha. When will you learn...? When will you choose the best part, like your sister—the part that endures forever?" [142]

Today, when visitors want to call, my "Mary" is fully in charge. I decline. I beg friends not to invite me places. Some become huffy; they don't get it. Experience says it's futile to share the best I know.

So not for the first time, a story from Hasidic scholar Martin Buber helps me say that I'm *wholly* occupied, completely caught up in this Christly state:

It's said that once upon a time a young rabbi went in search of his teacher whom he believed was in Paradise. By finding his master, he hoped to join him there.. Finally he spotted the elder, looking as ordinary as ever, wearing his old fur hat, sitting quietly on a rock where the path had ended. "Why that can't be Paradise![143]" exclaimed the student. Then came angels to clarify, "No, child. You've misunderstood. You thought your master was in Paradise, but in truth, Paradise is in your master."[144]

This casual contemplative has yet to find ways to say much about that state, that "peculiar," solitary joy. It's not simply uncommon. It's hidden stuff, this mostly set apart gladness. One enters the delight of belonging to God. [145] Talk intrudes on this peace. To repeat: This land is beyond both words *and* thought.

---

142. Luke 10: 38-42

143. In the New Testament, the concept of Paradise seems to have been supplanted by Heaven.

144. Martin Buber, *Tales of the Hasidim* (NY: Schocken, 1997), 180. (Greatly paraphrased).

145. Ephisians 1:14; 1 Peter 2:9

To be sure, some days my schedule is chatty, hectic, vexing, worrisome. I fret and fume and get easily irked. Sometimes, it's like O'Hare airport around here: cars and people come and go. My impatience to get back to work is palpable. But not today.

This day is a wonder. This day, I am simply joyful in the Silence. Today is pure pleasure: I'm completely free to simply abide in that secret place, to be "one-pointedly" with the Lord. No meetings, no dry-rot repair, no Fed X deliveries. The phone's ringer is off. Time is unstructured. My hours are only mildly organized.

This morning, I pray in the stillness of dawn—there's time enough for intercessory work. Two eggs over easy, then I can write. Soon I'll take a walk, maybe pull a few weeds or prune roses; the vines are heavy with pink fragrance. For lunch, I'll fix up a Pad Thai curry. In late afternoon, I'll have a dialogue session with a favorite client. What's not to love?

With or without my help, Love of the highest order increases itself.[146] How inexplicable this luxury in what some call "foolish things"—simple being, aimless puttering in the garden. With a warm sun on my back, and bees buzzing, it's quiet. I'm living in Silence, and into *the* Silence one day, I shall pass. For now, Wisdom builds her house. It's a dwelling place for God,[147] that I might live in Him, forever,—a partaker of the Glory that shall be revealed.[148]

ço

---

146. Eph. 4:16;Deuteronomy 14:2;

147. This concept and its imagery is developed so beautifully by Raimon Panikkar, *A Dwelling Place for Wisdom* (Louisville, KY: Westminster/John Knox Press, 1993).

148. Prov. 24:3; Ps. 23:6, 1 Peter 5.

ACKNOWLEDGEMENTS

Every book is, in one sense, a collaborative project. For this one, hearty thanks go to Mary Mobert who word-processed each chapter in its early, ever evolving stages. Her critical eye caught typos and editing issues I'd never noticed. Jon Sweeney edited my near-final draft. His suggestions greatly clarified my life's contemplative influences. Long time friend and gifted poet Fred Andrle proofed a completed version, spotting yet more nuances needing correction.

I am deeply grateful. Feeling compelled to tinker with a manuscript long after its final proofing, any errors are strictly my own.

AUTHOR'S BACKGROUND

Marsha Sinetar is an educator, corporate advisor on leadership, and bestselling author. A foremost advocate of the practical value of wholesome spirituality, her body of work is said to close the seeming gap between our material and spiritual life.

The Christian contemplative continues to develop leadership talent through her dialogue sessions. She works at home in the Pacific Northwest, living "as simply and quietly as possible."

Please visit: www.marshasinetar.com,
and her growing archive of talks on YouTube:
https://www.youtube.com/channel/UCVskCcoGDNerXWN6e7W0IJw.

INFORMAL SUBJECT INDEX

INFORMAL SUBJECT INDEX

CPSIA information can be obtained
at www.ICGtesting.com
Printed in the USA
BVHW052125261222
655031BV00021B/244